PENG

JUST LIK

John Lyall was born in Ilford, Essex, on 24 February 1940 and joined West Ham's office staff from school before becoming a professional player in 1957. He played just thirty-four first-team games for West Ham before a serious knee injury forced him to retire and concentrate on coaching. He became assistant manager to Ron Greenwood in 1971 and was promoted to team manager in 1974. In June 1989, following the club's relegation from the First Division, it was decided not to renew his contract.

Michael Hart joined the *Evening Standard* as a sportswriter in 1969 and was appointed chief football correspondent in 1976.

JOHN LYALL

with Michael Hart

JUST LIKE MY DREAMS

My Life With West Ham

PENGUIN BOOKS

PENGUIN BOOKS

Published by the Penguin Group
Penguin Books Ltd, 27 Wrights Lane, London W8 5TZ, England
Viking Penguin, a division of Penguin Books USA Inc.
375 Hudson Street, New York, New York 10014, USA
Penguin Books Australia Ltd, Ringwood, Victoria, Australia
Penguin Books Canada Ltd, 2801 John Street, Markham, Ontario, Canada L3R 1B4
Penguin Books (NZ) Ltd, 182–190 Wairau Road, Auckland 10, New Zealand

Penguin Books Ltd, Registered Offices: Harmondsworth, Middlesex, England

First published by Viking 1989
Published in Penguin Books 1990
1 3 5 7 9 10 8 6 4 2

Printed in England by Clays Ltd, St Ives plc
Filmset in Lasercomp Bembo

CONTENTS

PHOTOGRAPHIC ACKNOWLEDGEMENTS

Acknowledgement is gratefully given to the following for use of photographs:

Insert 1 (between pp. 88–9): *p. 4, top* – *Reynolds News*; *p. 6, top* – *Recorder Group*; *p. 7* – *Recorder Group*; *p. 8, top* – Steve Bacon; *p. 8, bottom* – *Daily Express*.

Insert 2 (between pp. 152–3): *p. 1, top* – Monte Fresco (*Daily Mirror*); *p. 1, bottom* – Steve Bacon; *p. 2, top* – Steve Bacon; *p. 2, bottom* – Steve Bacon; *p. 3, top* Steve Bacon; *p. 3, bottom* – Steve Bacon; *pp. 4–5* – Monte Fresco (*Daily Mirror*); *p. 6, top* – Steve Bacon; *p. 6, bottom* – *Stratford Express*; *p. 7, top* – Steve Bacon; *p. 8, top* – Steve Bacon; *p. 8, bottom* – Steve Bacon.

The publishers have made every effort to ascertain the copyright-holders of photographs but would be grateful to hear of any errors or omissions.

THE LAST DAY

Warm and radiantly sunny, Monday 5 June was much like any other day during the long, hot summer of 1989. The sun streamed through the bedroom windows of my house in the Essex countryside. I was already thinking over the problems I would face that day as I pulled on my clothes; problems faced by all football managers in the summer – pre-season friendly matches, training schedules and transfers. It was going to be a busy summer for me. On top of everything else that day was an appointment with the West Ham chairman, Mr Len Cearns, provisionally arranged nine days earlier. I had no idea what time I would be seeing him.

I had breakfast at my usual time, around 7.30 a.m. – tea, toast and cereal. I glanced through the *Daily Express* and, I guess like most managers, I looked at the back pages first. Bobby Robson, the England manager, was flying out with his squad that day to play a friendly match in Denmark. Apart from the usual injury stories and team speculation, there was little significant football news.

Yvonne, my wife, was going shopping that day. I told her that I'd be home for dinner around 6 p.m. I got in the car, a Mercedes provided by the club, and drove off to our training ground at Chadwell Heath, about ten miles away. It's an enjoyable drive through the fields and farmland, and gives me time to work out the day's schedule. Having just been relegated from the First Division I knew I would have to buy players and strengthen the squad that summer. But, more immediately, we had two reserve friendly matches to finalize, and the training programme had to be ready when the players returned from their holidays.

I was usually one of the first to arrive at the training ground. The players were on holiday and the only other people due in that day were the coaches and the catering staff. I had a cup of tea and sat down with one of the coaches, Tony Carr, and began discussing possible fixtures for the reserve team. When the telephone rang, Tony answered it. He called out: 'John, the chairman wants to talk to you.'

I went to the telephone. The chairman asked how I was and said he would like to see me at his house at 10 a.m. I said that I was awaiting calls from one or two managers – could he make it 10.30 a.m.? It was quite normal for me to visit the chairman. I had no idea what he wanted to see me about. He said he had something serious to discuss and I suspected it was connected with dealing in the club's shares.

For as long as I have known him, the chairman has been Mr Len, not just to me, but to all the staff and players. One of his brothers, also on the board of directors, has always been referred to as Mr Will. Mr Len and Mr Will, along with their late brother, Brian, a good friend to me, are the third generation of Cearns to serve on the board at Upton Park. Mr Len became a club director in 1948, and was elected vice chairman soon after the death of his father, W. J., in 1950. He succeeded Reg Pratt as chairman in May 1979.

Now a retired building contractor, he lives in a large, comfortable house in Chigwell, not too far from the club's training ground. It took me twenty minutes to drive there. I had always had a good relationship with him. I first met him when I was a young player at Upton Park, but, as with all players, you are rarely close to the directors. I began to get to know him better when I progressed to the coaching staff, but when he became chairman in 1979 – I was already manager – it was important for both of us that we worked well together. That was never a problem. He used to come into the club at least once a week, and although we sometimes had a difference of opinion we had great respect for each other. There was never interference from him; just discussion, opinion and advice. He was very fair in that way. He respected the professionals in the game. Looking back, we got along well together on the shop floor, but we had no relationship in the social sense. I think you have to separate your working and social life.

Well, Mr Len came to the door and showed me into the dining room. The dining room, like the house itself, was typical of Mr Len – solid, traditional, conservative. We sat either side of the large family dining table. It was the normal routine when I went to his house. He had papers laid out on the desk in front of him. I sensed that he was a little more tense than usual.

He came directly to the point. 'I'm sorry, John,' he said. 'But the directors have had a meeting and by a majority decision have decided not to renew your contract. I don't want to go into details. The decision is irreversible.'

To this day, I don't know who voted for me and who against.

Obviously, it was a shock. I had a four-year contract that expired that month. I'd had a contract since I became assistant manager to Ron Greenwood in 1971. But I had never automatically assumed they would renew any contract I'd had with the club. None the less, it was a surprise. It hadn't been a good season, I accepted that. Any manager whose team is relegated from Division One is vulnerable. That's football, and it will never change. But you tend to look at other factors, too, the balancing factors – your successes in the FA Cup and Littlewoods Cup, your loyalty, your long service, and the fact that the club probably made a profit that season of around £1.5 million. You hope that those sort of things will sway the balance in your favour.

In my case, obviously not. Even so, it was a decision I accepted automatically, because I believe that's par for the course in football. 'Fair enough, Mr Len,' I said.

I had no hint beforehand that they were about to relieve me of the job. There had been some speculation in the newspapers that I might move 'upstairs' into a new role as general manager. I don't know whether I would have accepted that situation. My thoughts until that moment had all been about preparing for the new season. Ron Greenwood, my predecessor as manager, had moved 'upstairs' – his own idea – allowing me to take charge of the first team. If they had offered me something similar I would have considered it.

But, at that moment, I felt there was no sense in debating the issue with Mr Len: he had said that the board's decision was irreversible.

He then said that the club wanted to make a statement to the Press. He had a prepared statement, handwritten on a piece of lined paper, which he pushed across the table towards me. It simply said that the board had decided not to renew the manager's contract and that Ronnie Boyce and Mick

McGiven would take over the running of the club on a temporary basis. It was concise, if not terse. He read it to me and asked if he could inform the news agencies that the statement had been agreed by us both. I said no. I wanted to be free to say what I wanted in my own time.

Inevitably, the atmosphere was difficult, strained. Suddenly we were looking at each other in a different light. We were no longer on the same side, sharing the same triumphs and defeats. It was a tense occasion for the chairman. We had known each other for a long time. Even so, I couldn't say that I noticed much sympathy, reluctance or any other emotion on his part, as he terminated my thirty-four years with the club. He was the chairman and he was accepting his responsibilities. He obviously believed that what he was doing was the right course of action for the club.

He asked if I would like twenty-four hours' grace before releasing the news. I declined the offer. 'You've made your decision,' I said. 'I think it should be made public immediately.'

'There is another option,' he then said. 'Would you like to resign?'

'No thanks, Mr Len,' I replied. 'If I've been dismissed, I've been dismissed.'

I felt that people should know the truth of the situation. Why try to disguise the truth? The club had made their decision, as was their right. If I had to live with the fact that I had been sacked, the club had to live with the fact that they had sacked me. It was not the traditional way of doing things at West Ham, but it was the truth of the matter, and it was important to me that people knew the truth.

Trying to hurry an unpleasant task along, the chairman

then moved quickly to the subject of compensation. He said that the club would like to reward me for the years of service I had given. They were offering, first, a lump-sum golden handshake, a further monthly payment until I got another job, three month's money in lieu of notice and, finally, a testimonial match.

I told him immediately that I didn't want a testimonial match. I felt the supporters of West Ham had done enough for me. I didn't want each of them dipping into their pockets for £5 for me. They owe me nothing. If anything, I feel I owe them all for the loyalty they have shown over the years. The chairman hadn't offered me my company car, so I said that instead of a testimonial match I would like to keep the car, and he agreed. I then told him that I would prefer to settle the financial details as quickly as possible, sever my connections with the club and get on with my life. I told him that a period of monthly payments while I was out of work didn't appeal to me. On the face of it, a regular payment of that nature seemed a warm gesture, but what if I was out of work for only a month. What would it have been worth to me then in cash terms? I said I would prefer one lump-sum payment. He said he would discuss it with the other directors.

We talked over the financial details for a few minutes more and then he said: 'What are you going to do now?' I told him I would like to go back to the training ground and break the news to the coaching staff. I asked him to give me an hour with them. He said he would talk to them himself later in the afternoon. There wasn't a lot left to say. He promised to call me within forty-eight hours to confirm the financial arrangements and, sure enough, two days later he telephoned the house to tell me that the matter was now in the hands of the club accountants.

In the end I received one lump-sum payment – about a year's salary – plus the Mercedes. It was satisfactory. I was out of contract and they were under no obligation to give me anything other than the statutory three months pay in lieu of notice. I don't think you can put a price on thirty-four years of service. Some managers, with far fewer years behind them, would have received a lot more, some a lot less.

The atmosphere in Mr Len's dining room was now stiff and formal. There was a long pause. 'OK, that's fine,' I said, and I got up from the table and left. If one thing upset me more than anything else, it was the fact that there was no personal acknowledgement or thank you from Mr Len. Perhaps he felt that sympathy might create an argument. Maybe he had it in his mind to say something like that but simply forgot in the tension of the occasion. I didn't get a cup of tea. We didn't shake hands. I left the table, walked out of the dining room and let myself out of the front door. In fairness, I think both of us probably felt the same – this is irreversible, let's get it over with and let's get out of here.

I closed his front door behind me and looked across the road at all the big houses, sitting proudly in the colour-supplement splendour of the Chigwell suburbs. It was a symbolic moment for me. I had just closed the door on thirty-four years of my life. 'Well, that's over,' I said to myself as I walked towards the car. 'What's next?'

I was upset, but not angry. In fact, my overwhelming feeling as I drove back to the training ground at Chadwell Heath was one of sadness. When I got back to the training ground, a place that had almost become a second home for me, Billy Bonds was supervising some youngsters who were painting the dressing room area. I called Bill into my little office, along with Tony Carr and Mick McGiven. I told them the news. They were stunned. Tony and Mick were particularly upset. Mick was in tears at one stage. I told them that I had enjoyed working with them. I told them to be sensible and do the job the chairman wanted them to do. I told them to do nothing silly: any hasty reaction on their part could affect the lives of their families. Finally, I told them the chairman would be visiting them that afternoon.

Ronnie Boyce and Eddie Baily, my chief scout, were on holiday. As Ron was at home, someone from the club called him with the news and asked him to see the chairman at the training ground in the afternoon. Eddie was in Scotland and called his daughter, Jane, by chance later that evening. She told him the news.

It was now lunchtime. I had spent less than an hour with the chairman. Suddenly, the matters of pre-season fixtures and training schedules were irrelevant. I said goodbye to the coaches, got in the car and drove home. On the way back I thought about the coaches, all loyal friends and all good at their jobs. I hoped the club would be fair to them. None of them had contracts. All could have been sacked along with me.

When I got home, Yvonne was out shopping, not expecting me back until 6 p.m. I had hoped to start my annual holiday the following day. I was taking three weeks off, my first break for twelve months. But I had booked to go away for only one week – fishing in Norfolk – because I envisaged a busy summer in the transfer market. I couldn't afford to be away for more than a week if I was trying to buy players. I intended to spend the other fortnight working from home.

My mind was quite clear. There was little point in looking back with regrets. I had to get on with my life.

It was early afternoon when Yvonne came home with the shopping. The club had issued a press statement by this time, but she had not heard the news. She came in the kitchen door carrying the shopping bags.

'What are you doing home so early? That's a nice surprise,' she said with a smile.

'I've lost my job,' I said.

She laughed. 'You're kidding me, aren't you?'

'Seriously, I've been sacked.'

She dropped the shopping bags on the floor. 'I can't believe it,' she said. 'They wouldn't do that to you. Would they?'

Like everyone else, she was hurt, shocked and upset – only more so. She sat down and we talked over a cup of tea. In many ways families give more to football than the managers do. The managers are doing something they want to do. For some it is almost an obsession. Wives and children are sometimes lonely because of the job we do. They don't get the same reward, the same sense of satisfaction. I found my job, every aspect of it, totally satisfying. Yvonne, on the other hand, found it a lonely experience at times. Her attitude that afternoon was simply: 'Well, I hope you now think it's all been worthwhile.' She has always been very protective towards me and I think she felt hurt after all the years of service I had given the club. I tried to put it all in perspective for her. 'We've got to look forward,' I said. 'At least we'll have more time together, for a while anyway.'

Yvonne called my mother and her parents but, unfortunately, my mother had seen the news on the lunchtime television. By this time the telephone was beginning to ring. I went upstairs, pulled on my jeans and went out into the back garden. I had been painting the upstairs windows. I got the paint pot out, put the ladder up to the windows and started painting. Life had to go on.

Within twenty minutes of climbing up the ladder, the phone was ringing incessantly. I was up and down that ladder for hours. Friends called, the Press called, a lot of players called ... Ray Stewart, Paul Hilton and Stewart Robson rang immediately. Graham Paddon called. Bobby Barnes called. Trevor Brooking called ... television's Brian Moore and Martin Tyler, as well as Ernie Gregory, the former West Ham goalkeeper who spent even longer with the club than me, all rang. One national newspaper immediately offered me £10,000 to tell my side of the story. I had never done that sort of thing and could see no point in doing it then.

Several managers called, including Alex Ferguson, Don MacKay, who said that if this could happen to me what chance had the rest of them, Jim McLean, and Tottenham's Ted Buxton, who called on behalf of Terry Venables, who was in the United States. Ron Greenwood, my former boss at West Ham, called with some consoling words.

Eventually, I gave up trying to paint. Ronnie Boyce came round to the house. He put his arm around Yvonne and said: 'I just can't believe it.' Tom Finn, the West Ham secretary, came round with a long-time friend and West Ham supporter Colin Wines. We were sitting in the garden talking when my son, Murray, came home. He's a carpenter and had been working inside a factory that day. He hadn't heard the news. He came through to the back garden, said 'Hello, Dad', and disappeared into the kitchen without realizing what had happened. Yvonne told him. The three of us talked later as a family. There was no point in feeling upset, angry or trying to fight back. We had to look forward. As a family we had always tried to keep football separate from our lives at home. If West Ham lost 5–0 I would return home knowing that my reception would be exactly the same as if we had won 5–0. That same family resolve re-emerged at that time.

To the Press that day I simply said that I was sad to be leaving the club and that I was grateful to the staff, players and fans for the support and loyalty I had received over the years. I felt I had to balance what had happened that day against a lifetime with the club. I didn't want to get the balance wrong, I didn't want to be bitter. Bitterness is a negative and destructive emotion, and I didn't want it gnawing at me for the rest of my life. One of the reasons I turned down the club's offer of a monthly payment while I was out of work was because it sounded a bit like charity to me. That didn't feel right, and I suspected that it would make me feel bitter. I decided when I closed the door at the chairman's house that I was going to be positive, not bitter.

That night we went to bed around 11 p.m. The telephone was still ringing. Paul Allen called just after we went to bed. Frank Lampard called about midnight. That was one of the nice things about the day. It was good to know I had so many friends in the game. I lay there with no real idea about what the future held for us. For the first time in thirty-four years I would wake up the next morning not working for West Ham. I had started the day much like every other during those years. I finished the day an unemployment statistic. Many people would have liked the chance to do what I had done over the previous thirty-four years. There was no bitterness or anger, just that feeling of sadness.

My experience that day made me determined to succeed

again as a manager. I felt I would like to go back to West Ham one day, as a rival manager, and win there convincingly. I felt at that moment that I would like to build a team as sound and as solid and as entertaining as some of those we had had at Upton Park.

It's very difficult to measure your success in football. Winning the League Championship is the ultimate achievement but, realistically, few clubs are capable of doing that these days. When Arsenal won the League title in 1989 they were only the fifth club to have done so in the last fourteen years. The rest of us? Well, we have to find the best means to survive. Then you ask yourself: How can I help my club not just survive, but thrive? At West Ham we always felt that the answer was to play attacking, entertaining football, with an element of risk. I like to think that most players I was associated with at the club enjoyed playing like that, and I like to think that most fans enjoyed watching it. That was Ron Greenwood's football philosophy, and I believe in it still. Perhaps, had West Ham not followed that philosophy, they may not have won the cup competitions and reached the finals that they did. Those were the kind of thoughts running through my head that night.

But I was chuckling to myself too. We hadn't eaten that day. Yvonne was preparing a lamb stew but we didn't feel hungry. It was just as well, she told me later, because she had forgotten to put the barley in it. It had been that kind of day.

My final memory of that day was of Graham Taylor, the manager of Aston Villa. He had called late in the afternoon. 'How are you, John?' he enquired. 'I want to sell you a player.'

'Graham,' I replied, 'I've got some news for you. I'd love to buy your player, but I've just been sacked.'

He was very apologetic, and later wrote me a beautiful letter, one of many I was to receive in the following days. It was a warm evening, but I slept well that night.

THE EARLY YEARS

I've always been positive, determined, perhaps a touch stub-born at times. As a manager you have to develop a degree of resilience, but obviously many of my characteristics were inherited from my parents. They both had a hard, early life in Scotland, and, although my own childhood was happy, I learned to appreciate that not all goals in life are achieved easily. I learned to take nothing for granted.

My mother, Catherine, was born in a crofter's village on the Isle of Lewis, off the west coast of Scotland. My father, James, came from the other side of Scotland – an old jute-weaver's town called Kirriemuir on the southern slopes of the Braes of Angus. My father was one of eight children. My mother was one of six.

If anything, life was more gruelling for my mother's family. Lewis and Harris, together with smaller islands, form the Outer Hebrides, a 150-mile-long storm break for the Western Highlands of Scotland. About 25,000 people live there, but the island nevertheless contains vast areas of empti-ness. It is mostly peat bog or rock. The winds are as cold as the sea, but the lonely white sands are spectacular. For my mother and her brothers and sisters, there were really only two options – stay on the island, cut peat, fish on the trawlers, join the Merchant Navy; or leave the islands and search for work on the mainland. Most of them chose to leave the islands – and all of them were successful in their lives. Her brothers Angus and Donald went to the United States, jumped boat, and later became business entrepreneurs. Roderick followed and went into the car business in Detroit. Angus later returned to the island and owned the local bus company with his brother John. My mum's only sister, Kate, established her own dressmaking business.

One of the traditions for the girls on the island was to go into service on the mainland. This is what my mother decided to do. She worked in a wealthy household in Edinburgh, and when that family moved to London she travelled down with them.

She was working in London when she met my father. Work was similarly difficult to find in Kirriemuir, a little town of sandstone cottages. There are still a few grain mills in the town, but it is noted mainly for the rich trout-fishing streams that flow into the Esk, and the fact that it was the birthplace of Sir James Barrie, who wrote *Peter Pan*. He was the son of a jute-weaver, and there is a house in the town preserved as a memorial to him.

My father was the second oldest of the eight children and originally worked as a carpenter, but he, too, moved to London and became a policeman. When he retired he was a sergeant stationed at Wanstead.

They were both solid Church of Scotland stock. They valued traditional family life. At Sunday lunch, at home in Ilford, Essex, my father always insisted on one of us saying Grace. They had left their own homes to secure their futures in London – that in itself must have been a daunting prospect for them – and they now valued what they had achieved. It was in no way luxurious or pretentious, but it was a very happy home. We lived above a shop in Ilford, and that was where I came into the world on 24 February 1940.

I sensed, even as a child, that my parents sacrificed their own comforts and little luxuries for the sake of their three sons – myself, Jimmy, who is three years older than me, and Roddy, who is five years younger than me. I think all three of us inherited our parents' determination. Jimmy, married with two children, is the managing director of a car company, and Roddy, married with three children, is a successful builder.

My parents gave all three of us a sense of responsibility. They taught us the value of integrity and hard work. And, in such an environment, we all grew to appreciate the rewards of a happy family life. They were strict and fair and gave us every opportunity to do what we wanted. My dad worked shifts in the police force but would come in from nightwork and still be prepared to take us out. We went out a lot, to cricket, speedway at West Ham, athletics, but mostly to football. That was the great love of my life from as early as I can remember.

The three of us were typical of youngsters in that part of London immediately after the war, but I remember my mother regularly pointing out to us that our dad was a policeman and, as such, we were expected to set an example. We all had a clip round the ear at some time or other but, basically, we were good kids who took our turns working the handle on the wringer on washing day.

Since those days, of course, I have become deeply involved with the youth of East London through football and West Ham, where we like to encourage the development of young players. Times have changed, standards have changed, but I think that was probably inevitable. When I was a kid, life was relatively simple. You went to school, you played football and cricket, and maybe you went to the cinema on Saturday mornings. There were few other options. We each had a little pocket money and you used to say to yourself: 'If I walk to the cinema I'll be able to buy an ice-cream, but if I take a bus I won't.' That was probably the biggest decision of the week. Compare that with the world kids have to wrestle with today. They have so many options it confuses them. They are far more worldly. Television has become a major influence on children today. It introduces them to a world we simply didn't know existed when I was young. So I think, on balance, our upbringing was a far easier, less fraught, process. We didn't face the temptations that children face today. We created our own entertainment. We were thrilled to bits if we were given an old set of pram wheels with which to make a trolley.

We created our own Wembley in the little alleyway at the back of the shop we lived above. It was here that, most days, we played football or cricket. Our favourite spot was a couple of doors along where the alleyway was wider. We played behind Mr Lorenzo's house. At that time Peter Lorenzo worked for the local weekly newspaper. When I had my first serious injury playing for West Ham he wrote an article about me in the paper. We became good friends, and years later, when he was a commentator with the BBC, he would joke that he first noticed the potential in me when I used the dustbins behind his house. I was very sad when he died at the tragically young age of 58.

I was about 7 years old when my elder brother, Jimmy, began taking me to the local park. He was a good player himself, and he used to push me to the park on the bicycle. I was always pleading for a game with the older boys. All the kids in those days were football fanatics. At first I was allowed only to stand behind the goal and run to fetch the ball when it went out of play. But I felt it was a privilege just to be involved with the older lads. One youngster I recall well. Dave Marr used to come to the park every Sunday morning with the ball tucked under his arm. The ball was spotless every week. He'd washed it, dubbined it, polished it, pumped it up and laced it perfectly. It was his pride and joy. About twenty of us gathered every Sunday, and he wouldn't let the ball touch the ground until the two teams had been organized. All the kids would shout: 'Come on, Dave, give us a kick', but the ball stayed under his arm until kick-off time. It was like a Cup Final every week, and by Friday all the local kids were speculating about the outcome of the big match. Initially I was no more than ball boy, but one day they let me play in goal and, finally, the moment came when I was a fully fledged team member. I was of average height but sturdily built. I was about 12 at the time. Looking back, I spent most of those early years playing football with older boys and, subsequently, I was always extending myself physically to match them. I grew to be quite a strong teenager and I wasn't easily intimidated.

I used to watch Tottenham and West Ham play on alternate Saturdays and occasionally went along to see the amateurs of Ilford. We took the 144 bus from Clayhall to the Angel, and then walked to White Hart Lane. I think my dad had a soft spot for Spurs. He particularly enjoyed taking me there for pre-season matches because they invariably played a Scottish club, and he used to say with great authority: 'I know these lads – I've seen them before.' I had been brought up on the great 'Blue Devils', the Scottish national team of whom my dad was inordinately proud. His particular hero was the legendary centre half George Young.

But Frank Whale, our next-door neighbour, was an avid follower of West Ham and would often say to me on a Saturday morning: 'Come on, John, I'll take you to see the Hammers.' He always stood on the same spot on the North Bank, and Ernie Gregory was his favourite player. Ernie, of course, was a wonderful goalkeeper, but he could do no wrong in Frank's eyes. Every time Ernie caught the ball Frank would say: 'Look at that John. The Cat, there are not many like him.'

As much as I enjoyed watching football, there was no substitute for playing the game. Every spare minute of each day was devoted to playing football. Regularly, for about six months of each year, I would return home covered from head to foot in mud. I must have been the muddiest boy in the street. My mum would often insist that I sat in the tin bath in the yard to wash before coming into the house. I washed my boots with just as much diligence. They were my pride and joy, and my mother knew it. I used to take the laces from the boots and wash them separately and then hand them to mother, who ironed them meticulously for me. As a youngster, I was a player who particularly loved tackling and slithering about in the mud. Both parents encouraged my enthusiasm for football, and one day, in the early fifties, they presented me with one of my most treasured gifts – a pair of Arthur Rowe boots. Arthur was manager of the great

Tottenham 'push and run' side that won the First Division title in 1951, and to have a pair of boots with his name on them was a real privilege enjoyed by few in our street. They were very expensive boots, and it underlined just how much my parents wanted the best for their sons.

Academically, I was above average, but I was no Trevor Brooking. He later went to the same school as me, but I was never in the same class, either on the football field or in the classroom.

I started my education at Parkhill Primary School in Clayhall. My future wife went to the same school, but we didn't know each other at the time. I was industrious enough as a pupil, but sport, and particularly football, was the great motivating factor in my life, even in those early days. I remember watching one of the teachers, Tom Carter, taking the older boys for soccer trials. I was a year too young to be a trialist, but I was happy to stand and watch. On this particular occasion, the ball flew out of play and I had the chance to return it. I really gave the ball a bang back on to the field, and Mr Carter must have been impressed. He called me over to him and asked if I played the game. 'Yes,' I said, 'but only in the park.' He asked me to join the trials the following week, and I guess that is when my career in organized football began.

Mr Carter was a big influence on me in those days, and years later we were friends. He wrote to me regularly as manager of West Ham, until he died a few years ago. He was a tall, kindly man who cajoled most of his young pupils through the 11-plus examination – me included. I think I might have been one of his tougher cases though, and I remember him using a little psychological blackmail to stress the importance of my academic studies. One day I was puzzled by an arithmetic problem. As usual my answer was wrong.

'I'm sorry, Sir, but I just can't do it,' I told him.

'You should remember the word "can't", John,' he said, 'because people who use that word never get anywhere in life. You don't think you *can't* play football do you? I'll strike a deal with you. I'll say you *can't* play football until you come back to me and say that you can do this problem. When you prove to me that you can do the problem I'll then say you can play football again.' He lectured me for thirty minutes that day on the dangers of negative thinking and the rewards of positive thinking. I've never forgotten what he told me. I solved the problem, passed the 11-plus – and played football.

At 11, I moved on to Ilford County High, where I came under the wing of Mr Percy Pyman, the PE teacher. He was a Football League referee and coached us in soccer and cricket. He was of a similar nature to Mr Carter – a conscientious coach and schoolmaster. Watching me play football, he recognized immediately that I was very left footed. 'If you want to learn to kick properly with both feet, play with a slipper on your left foot and a boot on your right,' he told me. I was that enthusiastic about the game that I was willing to try anything. It was worth it, because I was beginning to get noticed. I played for Ilford Schoolboys and remember with great affection the training sessions given by Stan Frankland, who is still involved with Essex schoolboy football. We used to travel from Ilford to Becontree for the District training sessions, and if you arrived late, Stan would say: 'You should have run here quicker.' He was a real enthusiast – he used to cycle alongside the lads during road runs – and also insisted that all his boys played and behaved properly on the field.

Football filled my life in those days, just as it does now. Every playtime, lunchtime and evening I was playing football. At school we stopped work for lunch at 12.15. I used to run out of the school gates, leap on a bus and take the five-minute journey home. Having bolted down my lunch, I took the next bus back to school so that I could devote the rest of the break to playing football. There was nothing else I wanted to do with my life other than to be a footballer. I think it caused my parents a few pangs of anguish, because it was not the most secure of professions and, in those days, even for the great players, not the best paid of professions either. Still, that was what I wanted to do with my life. The only other career that crossed my mind was that of a PE teacher. I knew I wanted an athletic, outdoor job. I didn't want to work in a factory or sit at a desk.

I was about 14 when these thoughts were formulating, and at that time I had the good fortune to come to the attention of Ted Fenton, a Forest Gate man who had been the manager of West Ham since 1950. John Cunningham, a schoolteacher friend of our family who had taught my elder brother and Ted's son Alan, had recommended me to West Ham.

Ted and Wally St Pier, West Ham's chief scout, watched me in two or three games, and finally made up their minds after a game at Walthamstow. It was March of my fourth year at Ilford County High. I was 15. At the end of the game I remember overhearing Ted say: 'Yes, we'll take him.'

Obviously my parents' first concern was about my education. Professional football was a high-risk business. Ted talked to my parents and explained the options. Essentially, these were just two. I could do what most young boys of my age did and go on the groundstaff. This meant I would work all week, sweeping the terraces, cleaning the boots or painting the stands, with the exception of Tuesday and Thursday afternoons, when I would train, and Saturday afternoons, when I would play. Or I could work in the office at Upton Park, continue studying at day-release school, and still train and play with the other lads. Ted suggested the second option and we agreed, though my parents were still unsure. My father went to see the headmaster at Ilford County High School, and he recommended that I stay at school. Otherwise, he felt, it was a waste of my education. He presented a lot of valid arguments against me leaving. It was a good school with a high academic reputation, and tradition demanded that pupils stayed on until the fifth year and achieved as high an education as possible. My parents listened to all the arguments. I think they felt I should stay at school; they felt I could be making the wrong decision. They were concerned for me and I understood that. Finally, one day, they relented. You are so determined to be a footballer, they said, that you would never forgive us if we didn't agree – and we believe you'll succeed.

So, I left school and, shining brightly and full of enthusiasm, reported for duty at Upton Park in June 1955. My first weekly wage was £4. Looking back, I have never regretted leaving school at 15, but it could easily have been so different. While I was unfortunate with injuries in my brief playing career in many other ways I had my share of good luck. As a manager I have often had to advise young players and their parents about the pitfalls of life in professional football. I have always been totally honest with them. I stress the importance of education. I always point out the risks involved, and I invariably relate my own experiences.

I always tell parents: 'You have to try to understand your son's feelings. I know, because I felt the same way at his age.' I present them with the options, warn them of the dangers, and let them make their own decision. I must have explained hundreds of times to parents what happened to my playing career when I was injured at 23. Looking back, I could have been finished with the game – and I had no significant educational qualifications.

Trevor Brooking did it the other way. He stayed on at Ilford County High School, achieved a high level of success with his examinations, and still had a wonderful playing career. But for me, as a 15-year-old, I felt at the time that West Ham's offer might be the only opportunity I would have to go into professional football.

So schooldays were over and family holidays were coming to an end too. The family used to go to Scotland each summer. My mother took the three boys for a month and my father usually followed us for the last two weeks. The journey to the Isle of Lewis could take almost two days by train and boat, but I loved going back to the island and still do. When my dad arrived we would travel across Scotland to his home town of Kirriemuir, where we would fish in the trout streams. That's probably where my love of fishing took root. Even there, though, we'd watch football. The season started a couple of weeks earlier in Scotland than it did in England and my dad used to take us to watch Dundee or Dundee United. I can remember seeing some great Scottish players, like Bill Brown, who later became the Tottenham goalkeeper, Billy Steel and Doug Cowie.

Once I began working at West Ham, though, the club and all it stood for became the priority in my life. I was determined to make a success of my career. The office work was not easy at times, and I found it difficult to concentrate. But, years later, what I learned was to prove invaluable. During the two years I worked in the office at Upton Park I learned how a football club – and particularly West Ham – was run. At the time, of course, I was happy to wade through the countless chores given me, simply because I knew that on Tuesday and Thursday afternoons I would be able to train and on Saturday afternoons I would be able to play.

West Ham was a very friendly club. It fostered a community spirit and was deeply loyal to the old retainers. We were rather like one big happy family. Frank Cearns had been appointed secretary in 1946 and was still running the administrative side of the club. He was a member of the Cearns family that had helped control the fortunes of West Ham since W. J. Cearns was appointed chairman in 1935. He shared a secretary with the manager, Ted Fenton. She was one of the most loyal retainers – Mrs Pauline Moss, who apart from being secretary to Ted and Frank, was later secretary to Ron Greenwood and Eddie Chapman. Eddie had joined West Ham shortly after Frank. He was essentially a player, and one with a big future, but, after being demobbed, he combined the duties of playing with those of helping out in the office. He was later, of course, to become West Ham's long-serving club secretary, but in those days he was assistant secretary, and the fact that we were both players gave us plenty to talk about.

But it was Mrs Moss who I was closest to. She taught me virtually all I know about office administration. On my first day she had me answering the telephone, and if I didn't speak with the correct degree of politeness she was quick to scold me. 'You were a bit curt, John,' I remember her telling me. She wrote all the confidential correspondence for the club manager and secretary, and I remember her showing me how to prepare a business letter. When I was typing she would often tell me I was pressing the keys too hard. The busiest days in the office were just before FA Cup ties, when I had to stamp out all the tickets and address the envelopes. It was all invaluable experience, but I played football at every opportunity. Frank Cearns understood how I felt and would often, if I was kicking about downstairs with the groundstaff boys at the end of my lunch, allow me a few extra minutes. I had no way of knowing what was to develop later in my career at West Ham, but those two years in the office prepared me for some of the administrative routine I would face in management.

Twice a week, of course, training came to the rescue. I enjoyed training almost as much as I enjoyed playing. I joined the other groundstaff boys, but particularly remember training with three cricketers – Doug Insole, Mickey Stewart and Frank Rist. Doug and Mickey played for Corinthian Casuals in the winter, and Rist and Stewart both played briefly for Charlton Athletic. I played quite a bit of cricket during the summer months, for my school and District and a couple of times for Essex Club and Ground. I used to bat and keep wicket. In those days young professional footballers still had the time in the summer to play cricket. We had a few cricketers at West Ham, like Geoff Hurst and Eddie Presland, who both played county level for Essex, and Bobby Moore. Ted Fenton was an enthusiastic and useful cricketer, too. He played for Clayhall and a team called Ilford Thursdays.

During the summer months, if it was quiet in the office, he'd give me the afternoon off and I'd go and play for the Ilford team.

I suppose those two years passed quickly enough. I attended day-release school, trained hard, played hard and listened and learned. Bill Robinson, who was assistant manager to Ted, often took me to one side after a game and quietly explained what I was doing wrong. He used to watch me play for the third team, and he was particularly critical of my heading. So I worked at it. I must say, though, that he was first to pat me on the back if I had a good game. I had a great affection for Bill and still do. He came from Whitburn in the north-east and was as hard as nails. But he was also a very fair and funny man. He had played for Sunderland and Charlton – he won an FA Cup winner's medal with them – before joining West Ham. He was a powerful and intimidating centre forward, very popular with the Upton Park fans. When his playing career ended he took charge of the junior teams and later became Ted's assistant.

Bill often popped into the office and he always had a word of encouragement – and a joke. I remember in 1956, after we drew 3–3 in an FA Cup sixth-round tie at Tottenham, busily wading through ticket applications for the replay. We worked through Sunday and Monday processing the replay tickets for our 4,000 season-ticket holders; it was my job to despatch them. The usual procedure was to take them to the main post office at East Ham, and I was about to struggle out with two enormous sacks of tickets when Bill walked in.

'I'll help you,' he said, and as we set off out of the ground he added: 'Listen. Let's just walk up to the pillar box round the corner and post them there.' I was a bit doubtful, but he was the man in authority, so we walked up, beyond the Boleyn pub, to the little pillar box. I stood in front of the box, pushing the letters through, while Bill stood with the sacks, giving me fistfuls of envelopes at a time. Suddenly, he was no longer handing me the envelopes.

'Come on, Bill,' I said. 'We've got loads of these to get through.' I looked round. Bill was twenty yards away, whistling innocently to himself. Standing the other side of me was the postman – not looking very happy. He proceeded to explain to me why I should not put so many letters in a small box.

As manager of the junior teams, Bill worked closely with Wally St Pier, the club's chief scout, who was to establish a legendary reputation for discovering young talent. Like me, Wally had a brief playing career at West Ham, but he was part of the family and became one of the best known scouts in the game. He was a large, powerful man, with a very firm handshake and a warm smile. He did deep breathing exercises every day before leaving home in Romford, and would then walk to work. 'Done your exercises today, boy?' he used to ask me most days.

Wally, Ted, Bill and the club chairman at the time, Reg Pratt, together with part-time staff, were chiefly responsible for formulating the youth policy that was to bring such success to Ron Greenwood's managerial reign a few years later. The country was still rebuilding after the war, but there were signs of affluence ahead. Youngsters were more active, more demanding. They were searching for new challenges. I think West Ham were one of the first clubs to capitalize on this growing trend. But they were not the only club. Chelsea were already developing a fine young side, and they had snatched from under the noses of West Ham one of the best young players of the era – Jimmy Greaves, who I had played against when he was a Dagenham Schoolboy. Manchester United already had a great young side – The Busby Babes. I had personally experienced the depth of talent they had at Old Trafford. In 1957 I played in the West Ham side that met Manchester United in the FA Youth Cup Final. They had a superb side, including two players with first-team experience – the goalkeeper David Gaskell and the centre forward Alex Dawson. They beat us 8–2 over two legs.

It was a disappointment, but Mr Pratt and Ted considered reaching the final to be confirmation of the wisdom of a sound youth policy. Within a matter of a few years the club was bursting at the seams with outstanding young players – Bobby Moore, Tony Scott, Mickey Beesley, Andy Smillie, Eddie Bovington, Johnny Cartwright, Michael Brooks, Geoff Hurst, Ronnie Boyce, Eddie Presland, Noel Cantwell, John Bond, Martin Peters, Kenny Brown, Mike Grice, John Sissons, Joe Kirkup . . . the list was never-ending. A group of us became firm friends – myself, Joe Kirkup, Bobby Moore, Harry Cripps, Andy Smillie, Bobby Keetch, Mike Grice and Tony Scott. Later, Geoff Hurst, Martin Peters, Ronnie Boyce, Joe Kirkup and myself, with wives and girlfriends, used to go out together. We spent a lot of time together, and frequently ended up after training sharing a pot of tea in an Italian café just round the corner from the ground.

Cassetari's was a favourite haunt for West Ham players at the time. It was a family run café, and they used to let the senior and young players sit upstairs and talk about football. None of us knew it at the time, but a high percentage of the lads who sat talking football in that little café went on to

become coaches and managers. Among my playing con-
temporaries who progressed into coaching, management and
administration were Phil Woosnam, who was to become
Commissioner of the North American Soccer League,
Malcolm Allison, John Bond, Ken Brown, Bobby Moore,
Malcolm Musgrove, Geoff Hurst and Martin Peters. We all
learned from Ted, and later, of course, from Ron Greenwood.
As a youngster I didn't have too much contact with Ted on a
day-to-day basis, but he was always very considerate. I
showed him the respect he deserved and realized that, as
manager of the club, he had priorities other than the career of
John Lyall. But, as I progressed from youth to reserve level, I
was more involved in his coaching sessions and began to
realize that he was an excellent trainer of players. He had
been an army PT instructor in Africa and Burma during the
war, and he knew how to make training interesting. There
was little coaching as we know it today, but Ted was an
innovator. He invariably worked out a little team plan before
an FA Cup tie to help motivate the players. He tried to vary
training routines, and I remember him introducing rugby,
which I found quite enjoyable until Malcolm Musgrove
stuck his fingers in someone's face as he tried to tackle him.
He was also one of the first managers in the country to
introduce the cut-away Continental boot. I think the changes
he instituted provided the foundations for West Ham's success
in the decade that followed.

At this time I was playing mostly in West Ham's 'A' and 'B'
teams, and I came to realize the benefit of playing alongside
older, more experienced men. One such was Dick Walker,
who had a 25-year playing career with West Ham, interrupted
only by wartime service in the Parachute Regiment.

Dick retired in 1957, but not before he had taught me a few tricks in the third and reserve teams. He was a shrewd man, and before a game he used to point me out to the referee and say: 'Look ref, I don't want those old pros on the other side kicking that young lad. He's only 16 you know.' He taught me a great deal and was a big influence in my early career as a player. As a youngster, it was important for me to get stuck in and get involved, and if I failed to do that he would tell me: 'John, if you don't pass the ball quickly and compete, you won't have a chance.' I was learning to be strong, and like everyone else I made bad tackles unintentionally, but I was never cautioned or sent off. The referee just said 'Watch it, son', and you heeded the warning in those days, whether he was right or wrong.

Eventually, Joe Kirkup, Bobby Keetch, Tony Scott and myself got the chance to play regularly in the reserves. They originally put me in the side at left half, but when Freddie Cooper left the club in 1958 I was moved to left back – and that's where I stayed. Just before that, in February 1957, I won my only significant representative honour – an England Youth cap. I was selected to play for England against Luxembourg at Upton Park. We won 7–1, and Jimmy Greaves scored four goals. I remember that match particularly, not just because it was my only international honour, but because I hoped that my elevation to England status would impress a young lady I had met at a bus stop. Yvonne was a secretary in the City, had attended the same primary school and lived just three roads from me. We regularly met at the bus stop, but it took me a while to pluck up enough courage to talk to her. She was a very attractive girl, and one day, having rehearsed the line several times, I said: 'Good morning. How are you today?'

She quite obviously didn't consider me a matinée idol, so I knew I would have to come up with something better than that. The Football Association came to the rescue with the letter informing me that I'd been selected to play for England. That morning I met her at the bus stop.

'Good morning,' I said. 'How are you today? I've been selected to play for England.'

'Oh, thrilling!' she said. Still, I must have done something right. We became engaged in February 1959, on my nineteenth birthday, and married two years later. We bought a house in the Essex village of Abridge for £2,775.

By this time I was aware that I had a problem with my left knee. In December 1958 Ted told me that he was thinking of giving me my first-team debut against Manchester City at Maine Road. Unfortunately, I hurt my knee, and Joe Kirkup played instead. It was just the beginning of my problems. The following season, my first as a full professional, I was scheduled to make my first-team debut against Millwall in a Southern Floodlit Cup match. I was named in the team, but that morning my father, who was in Scotland to attend a family funeral, had a heart attack. At one stage it was feared he might die, so I withdrew from the team because I wanted to be with my mother in Scotland. Typical of Ted Fenton and the club, my wage packet that week contained £38. My usual wage was £14, but they had paid me the first-team appearance and bonus money.

I eventually made my first-team debut in February 1960, against Chelsea at Upton Park. Ted had a lot of problems with injuries at the time. He was planning to play Noel Cantwell, a defender, at centre forward, but he failed a fitness test. John Bond, another defender, moved to centre forward,

Joe Kirkup played at right back and I played at left back. I was apprehensive – and rightly so.

My first task on my debut in Division One – Ted had steered the club to the Second Division Championship in 1958 – was to mark Peter Brabrook. He was a fast, cunning outside right who had played for East Ham and Essex Schoolboys and was now an England international. A 29,000 crowd had squeezed into Upton Park for this big London derby, and it was my first taste of the big-match atmosphere. It was a special day in my career, but I remember my stomach churning in the dressing room before the game.

Peter, who later played for West Ham, gave me all kinds of problems. At half time I recall Noel Cantwell coming into the dressing room with a few words of advice for me. 'If you don't get a good tackle in he will run you off the park,' he said. So, in the first minute of the second half, I slid into him like an earth-moving machine with a perfectly timed challenge. From that point on, as Noel Cantwell pointed out, I was dictating the play in the little duel between us. I felt much more confident after making that challenge. Tackling was always the big strength in my game.

We filed off the pitch at the end having won 4–2, and I can remember feeling ten feet tall. 'Well, maybe I've arrived at last,' I thought. Ted Fenton, of course, put all that euphoria into perspective. I had done well enough, he said, but no more than that. He knew, and I was to learn, that managers need patience and tolerance when nursing youngsters through the early stages of their careers.

However, it was a good start and a good win, thanks largely to a hat-trick from our makeshift centre forward John Bond. A right back and penalty expert, he none the less deputized at times in a striking role with some success. A few days before my debut, West Ham had played Arsenal at Highbury in a friendly match. I played along with two other youngsters, Tony Scott and Mickey Beesley.

I remember that match for two reasons. It was the first time West Ham wore their white strip with the claret and blue hoops. The second reason – John Bond's spectacular 30-yard shot that gave us a 1–0 win at Highbury.

Noel Cantwell returned to the side for the next First Division game, against Newcastle, but I was back for the following match – a 3–1 defeat by Nottingham Forest. Seven minutes from half time in that match I twisted my knee and was stretchered off. I didn't play another first-team match that season. It wasn't until the following season – 1960–61 – that I began to consider myself a relatively regular first-team player. I'd spent the first two months of the season in the reserves, and the first team's form had been indifferent. When Noel Cantwell was injured, Ted decided to put me back in the side against Blackburn Rovers at Ewood Park. At the time, Rovers were one of the most exciting teams in the First Division, and the man I was to mark, Bryan Douglas, was an experienced England international and one of the best wingers in the game. The match couldn't have started more painfully for me. After just six minutes I challenged Douglas for a high ball, we clashed heads and I broke a tooth. I was knocked out. I had a bruised lip, throbbing gum and slight concussion. Bill Jenkins, the team physiotherapist, finally revived me on the pitch, and I insisted that I stay on the field. I was a little groggy for the rest of the first half, but after the interval I chased and harried Douglas relentlessly, and over the ninety minutes, I won on points. In fact, I finished the game something of a hero. I was fortunate enough to make a good interception eight minutes from time and, from my pass, Malcolm Musgrove set up a chance for John Dick to score the winning goal. It was 3–2 and I was the proudest man on the pitch.

I have a newspaper cutting that I have treasured to this day. The headline reads: 'Lyall Dims England Star.' To be honest, there were few headlines like that.

Three days after the match, I had the remains of the broken tooth removed and a false one installed. I kept my place in the side against Birmingham City the following week – a 4–3 win – and altogether played twenty-one First Division games that season. I think because of the impression I made in those early games the club decided to accept Manchester United's bid of £29,500 for our regular left back Noel Cantwell. At the time it was a British record fee for a full back. He had lost his place to me originally because of injury and then couldn't get back into the side. In a way I was sorry to see him go. He was the captain of the Republic of Ireland, a superb professional, full of life. I used to play cricket with him in the summer, and we'd sometimes enjoy a drink together. But next day, if we were training, he'd have the heavy gear on and he got down to business. He knew how to enjoy himself, but he knew how to work, too. It was sad to see him leave Upton Park, but his departure opened the door to the first team for me. By the end of that season I was full of confidence and optimism.

My sense of well-being was completed that April, when Murray was born. Yvonne went into labour in the middle of the night, and my car, a Morris Traveller Estate, was in the garage with the battery on charge. Fortunately, it started, and I got her to the hospital in time. It had been a good season for me. But it was to be my only good season as a player.

At the beginning of April that season, Ted Fenton, who had been a great help to me, left the club in circumstances that have never been fully explained. I didn't know what had happened. As is often the case, the players rarely know the real reasons behind a manager's departure. I was just 21 and as surprised as anyone. Looking back, I can draw a parallel with my own situation, because the players under me at West Ham would have had little knowledge of the circumstances of my departure. At the time of Ted's departure the first team had won only one of the previous fourteen games. We finished the season in sixteenth place in Division One. Ted never spoke afterwards about what had happened, but I remember a story in the *Ilford Recorder* at the time stating that he had been allowed to resign rather than be sacked.

Ron Greenwood was appointed manager shortly afterwards, and he was the first manager to have had no previous connection with the club. He chose Joe Kirkup and John Bond as his regular full backs the following season, and I played just four first-team games. But by this time it was becoming obvious that there was a serious weakness in my left knee. I'd had my first ligament operation at the age of 18, but it hadn't solved the problem. I spent most of the next three seasons in and out of the reserves, in hospital or on the treatment table at Upton Park, where Bill Jenkins, whose son Rob was to succeed him when he passed away suddenly, worked diligently to prepare me for matches. It got to the stage where I wasn't really concerned about the level of my performance on the playing field; I was more concerned with completing the ninety minutes. In one come-back match against Arsenal in the Southern Floodlit Cup, a Tommy Docherty tackle sent me straight back to the treatment room.

A few weeks later I had my first knee operation. When Jackie Burkett, a fine left back, staked a regular place in the first team in 1962–3 displacing Joe Kirkup and relegating me to third choice, my future was beginning to look increasingly gloomy.

I was good enough to do the job; I had no doubt about that. I had just about enough qualities and, had it not been for the weakness in my left knee, I think I could have made a career as a professional footballer. I battled on, though, and didn't begin to feel disillusioned until my last season. In the first game of the season 1963–4, I played in the reserves against Tottenham. I remember turning sharply and the knee immediately coming out of joint.

I had treatment for six weeks, began training, and, in my second game back, the knee went again. It would lock out of joint and I couldn't release it. I had another operation, trained, felt really strong and played in a come-back match against the Metropolitan Police at Imber Court in Surrey. I hadn't felt so good for a long time. Ron Greenwood, by this time well-established as manager, was there to watch the game. I played a ball with the outside of my foot and suddenly my knee popped out of joint again. It was a devastating moment for me. 'It's no good,' I thought. 'I just can't do it.'

That was my last attempt at a come-back. It was January 1964, one month short of my twenty-fourth birthday. I knew then that my career as a professional footballer was over. I had played just thirty-five First Division games for West Ham. The injury was finally diagnosed as a generally disarranged knee. It was inoperable, irreparable.

I left the pitch at Imber Court ten minutes from the end of

the game. Ron Greenwood came into the dressing room and we sat alone. 'The knee's just no good,' I told him. 'There's no point in going on.' Ron told me not to make a decision at that moment. He told me to take a year off in the hope that the rest would cure the problem. I didn't feel I could do that. I felt instinctively that the knee would never be right. Ron was very sympathetic. He sent me to different specialists for more treatment – but I knew I would never play again.

Of course, I was worried about the future. I had a wife, a son and a mortgage, but not once did I regret becoming a professional footballer. It had been a brief career, but I enjoyed every moment of it – apart from the injuries. Ron said the club would obviously keep me until my contract expired that June. At least that gave me a few months' breathing space.

Then, most significantly, West Ham began to string to-gether a run of good results in the FA Cup. In the month I was injured at Imber Court, we beat Charlton Athletic and Leyton Orient to progress to round five. We beat Swindon Town 3–1, and by the time we beat Burnley 3–2 in the sixth round, Ron, I was told, was using my injury as part of his team talk. He was telling Bobby Moore, Geoff Hurst, Martin Peters, Johnny Byrne and Peter Brabrook how fortunate they were compared to me. He would tell them that a trip to Wembley for the FA Cup Final would ensure a bumper testimonial match for me at the end of the season.

As the cup-run developed, Ron began sending me to watch the opposition, and I enjoyed the involvement. In March we beat Manchester United 3–1 at Hillsborough to reach the final, and Ron called me into his office. He said he had consulted the players and they all wanted me to organize their FA Cup Final pool, which traditionally provides the players with perks from newspapers and promotions. I was delighted to do that, and set up my office in the club's press room.

I raised some money for the players, but it was nothing like the revenue from my testimonial match at the end of the season. Ron organized it for the Monday of FA Cup Final week which, I recall, provoked a little controversy in the newspapers, coming just five days before we were due to play Preston North End at Wembley. But it was a typical gesture by Ron, who always treated the welfare of his players as a priority. That night Ron fielded his FA Cup Final team against an All Stars line-up that included Terry Venables and several ex-Hammers, like Noel Cantwell, Johnny Dick, Malcolm Musgrove and Phil Woosnam. West Ham won 5–0, Geoff Hurst scoring four of them, and a crowd of 18,000 paid gate receipts of £3,590 and £207 for match programmes. That was a lot of money in those days. Considering that my contribution as a player had not been very significant, the actions of the club and the fans that night underlined the strong sense of loyalty that existed at Upton Park. I was full of gratitude, but the club avoided portraying that evening as something unusual. It was the West Ham way of doing things.

I still knew though that by June I would be out of work. I was wondering what to do with my life, when an offer came along to coach children at Stepney School five afternoons a week. At least that was one source of income. Then Eddie Chapman told me he was looking for a part-timer to organize the wages department at Upton Park, so I asked him if I could work five mornings a week, and he agreed. I couldn't believe my good fortune. Perhaps I wasn't going to be a great footballer, but at least I could support my family.

Then, just before the FA Cup Final, Ron called me into his office. 'I want to use you next season,' he said. It transpired that the club's part-time youth team manager, Tom Russell, a schoolteacher from Leyton, had taken a new post in Uganda. Suddenly, I was West Ham's youth team manager – and inundated with job offers. I was just lucky, though I had struck a rapport with Ron. I admired him as a man and an outstanding coach, and most of what I have learned in football has come from him. His words of advice gave me a tremendous insight into coaching.

Soon after he had taken over as manager at Upton Park, we played a First Division match at Tottenham, and I was due to mark Cliff Jones. He was a terrific little winger. He had pace, was comfortable running with the ball, was brave at the far post, and as capable of scoring a goal as any central striker. Most wingers in those days tended to confine themselves to the line and the wide areas of the pitch, but Cliff loved to be in the thick of the action with a bold diving header at the back post. Anyway, before that game, Ron said to me in the dressing room: 'One thing about Jones – he likes to turn with the ball. If you're too tight he'll murder you, just hang off him a little.'

I did just as Ron advised, and the little Welsh wizard had one of his quieter afternoons. At the end of the game I remember people patting me on the back and saying 'Well done, John.' I was delighted with myself. I took the credit but knew that without Ron's foresight I might not have had such an enjoyable game. That experience, and similar ones, taught me the value of sound coaching advice.

If Cliff Jones was one of the best players I marked, the man I most enjoyed playing alongside was, without question, Bobby Moore. He was a dream to play with. He spoke to you every minute of the game. When the ball arrived at your feet he invariably told you where to play it next. He had time to play your game as well as his own – and that's the greatest compliment you could pay him. He was a Barking lad and a good friend of mine. We had grown up together. When he first came to Upton Park he was a good player, but no more outstanding than some of the others. But he had a thirst for knowledge and he was a prodigious trainer. But, just as his wonderful career took root, mine was aborted by the knee injury.

On FA Cup Final day I sat on the substitutes' bench at Wembley and watched him in action – imperious, aloof, commanding, composed. I wasn't in the same class as a player, but I could have been out there, dogged, muscular, resolute, determined.

It was a poignant day for me. West Ham beat Preston 3–2 and I was delighted for the lads. But my dream of becoming a great player was over. I wasn't sure what the future held in the long term but, whatever I did, I was determined to make a success of it.

THE FAMILY CLUB

I could have been a youngster on the scrapheap, a familiar enough conclusion to so many fledgling careers. Instead, the family traditions of West Ham had come to my rescue. I sat at Wembley that day, watching the unfolding drama on the field, wishing I had been part of it but knowing at the same time that I had been fortunate. I could have been finished with football. In reality, though, I was only just beginning.

I had played with most of the West Ham team that appeared in the 1964 FA Cup Final: Jim Standen, John Bond, Jackie Burkett, Eddie Bovington, Ken Brown, Bobby Moore, Peter Brabrook, Ronnie Boyce, Johnny Byrne, Geoff Hurst and John Sissons. A common thread ran through that team. With the exception of Standen and Byrne, they were all either born or brought up in the London or Essex areas. There existed a great sense of unity and team spirit, and there was a strong local identity with the supporters. This team was the product of the youth policy which had taken root a few years earlier under Ted Fenton. I could have been part of it. But it wasn't to be. I was, though, still part of the family, and I was grateful for that.

I started work the following season under Ron Greenwood. I was the youth team manager, part-time of course. In the mornings I worked as the wages clerk at Upton Park. In the afternoons I worked with the children at Stepney School, and the rest of the time I devoted to coaching youngsters at West Ham. Among the first group of lads I had at West Ham were Trevor Brooking and Frank Lampard. Trevor, being a particularly bright boy, was still at school. Frank was on the staff. Even at that age it was obvious they had the quality to go a long way in the game. We instilled in boys like that a sense of loyalty that survives to this day. You didn't have to be at the club long to understand how consciously the club tried to foster the sort of loyalties that are involved in a family. There have been only six managers and six secretaries in the history of the club. No other club in the Football League can match that kind of stability. Former West Ham players have filled almost all the positions as managers, coaches, scouts and, in the case of Eddie Chapman, who spent nearly fifty years with the club, as secretary too. Ron Greenwood and my successor, Lou Macari, are the only two managers who had not previously been with the club as players. This continuity can be traced back to the beginning of the century. Five local men, who served on the board in 1904, were still there fifteen years later when the club made the decision to join the Football League.

The history of the club makes fascinating reading and I would recommend that anyone with a serious interest reads a book called *West Ham United: The Making of a Football Club* (Duckworth, 1986), written by Charles Korr. As far as I know, it is the only detailed history of the club that has been published. Charles is an American history professor, and I thought it quite remarkable that the board of directors should open their archives to him. But they did, and during the course of his research we became friends. He was one of the first people to telephone me after I had been sacked.

His book tells how Arnold F. Hills, owner of the Thames Ironworks, created the Thames Ironworks Football Club. He was a militant temperance advocate, a vegetarian and a believer in crusading for good causes. Educated at Harrow and Oxford, he had been the English mile champion and had also played football. He was a kindly employer who started a number of leisure pursuits for his workers, including a string band, a drama club and, of course, the football club. He was concerned about the overcrowding in the east end of Victorian London and the fact that the local children had to play football in the spaces squeezed between factories and rows of terraced houses. The football club was started in 1895 and, to this day, the Hills family remain the club's major shareholders.

In 1900 Hills severed the club's formal connections with the Ironworks shipyards, proposed that the club became a limited company, and became the biggest shareholder. Four years later, the club took its most significant decision, moving from its first home – The Memorial Ground in the docklands – to its present Boleyn Ground, originally a vegetable garden owned by the Catholic ecclesiastical authorities. From that time onward, the tone of West Ham United was set. Charles Paynter, a player with the club since 1900, was to become manager in 1931 and retire in 1950 after half a century of service. His successor was Ted Fenton. Syd King, a former player, was appointed secretary in 1901 and served as secretary-manager until his death in 1931, when Paynter took over.

From the beginning of the century the hallmark of West Ham has been continuity. J. W. Y. Cearns was a founding member of the club and a director who served, apart from a three-year break, from 1900 until his death in 1934. Ten years before he died, two new members were co-opted to the board – W. J. Cearns and F. R. Pratt. Cearns was the son of J. W. Y. Cearns, and F. R. Pratt, a local timber merchant, was his friend and business associate. They and their families became the backbone of the club. W. J. Cearns served on the board for twenty-six years until his death, and was chairman from 1935 to 1950. F. R. Pratt remained on the board until his death in 1941. He was succeeded on the board by his son R. H. (Reg) Pratt. In 1948 Cearns' son L. C. (Len) Cearns joined the board. For most of this century there has been at least one member of the Cearns family on the board and, since 1924, there has always been a member of the Pratt family on the board too.

W. J. Cearns, Len's father, began his professional life as a junior clerk but eventually founded his own construction and engineering company. He built the first concrete stands at West Ham, and anyone who enters the Boleyn Ground today is surrounded by steel and concrete monuments to W. J. Cearns. His son, Mr Len, and Mr Pratt were both to become significant influences on my career at Upton Park. Mr Pratt, who became chairman in 1950 and served in that position for twenty-nine years, was the man who steered West Ham into the modern era and, at the same time, preserved and enhanced the traditions of the club.

As a young man at Upton Park I had little contact with him, but I was aware of the close business relationship he established with Ron Greenwood. They worked well together, and I know that Ron had a very high regard for the chairman. The chairman held his relationship with the manager to be one of the most important aspects of his job. He was a caring man. He and Ron developed such a good understanding and sense of trust and loyalty that I was fortunate enough to inherit a similar relationship when I took over as manager. It wasn't until 1971, when Ron appointed me as assistant manager, that I began to get to know Mr Pratt well. Like his father, he was a timber merchant who lived in Wanstead. He was a local JP and had a charming wife, Gwen, who always enquired about Yvonne and Murray.

During the latter part of my role as assistant manager, Ron felt I should attend the board meetings at Upton Park. At that time I felt it was a privilege, and it was all part of the learning process. By the time I was manager and had to make a report to the board and give my observations, I knew the routine. It was an invaluable experience for me. At West Ham the manager is treated almost like a member of the board of directors. The tradition is that he stays in the boardroom for the entire meeting. At most other clubs the manager gives his report and leaves. In those days, back in the seventies, the boardroom at West Ham, like most in football, was wood-panelled, and the directors sat in leather-padded chairs around the boardroom table. Mr Pratt's chair, of course, had a slightly higher back than the other chairs.

Mr Pratt protected the club's traditions diligently. He had sound opinions about football and believed the game should be played the right way. But at the same time he was a competitor. He wanted to be successful and he didn't like losing, but he kept the game in perspective. He was a gentleman, too. When I was manager he used to come to the club most Tuesdays. I would be sitting in my office around lunch time and he would knock softly on the door. 'Have you got a minute, John,' he used to ask. He would walk in, smiling, sit down and say: 'Well, the least you could do is offer me a sherry.' I liked Mr Pratt very much.

He was a fatherly figure to both Ron and I, but not in the patronizing sense. He was a friend and he could be firm when necessary. He would invariably accept the decisions of both Ron and I as managers on matters of football policy, but in other areas he had his own mind and he made his own decisions. I particularly remember the drama that engulfed the club in January 1971 after Blackpool had beaten us 4–0 in the third round of the FA Cup. On the night before the game, Bobby Moore, Jimmy Greaves, Clyde Best, Brian Dear and physiotherapist Rob Jenkins were spotted drinking in the Blackpool nightclub owned by former British heavyweight boxing champion Brian London. Their misdemeanour was leaked to the newspapers, and the publicity, combined with the fact that West Ham were comprehensively beaten, meant that Ron Greenwood had to take severe disciplinary action. I remember him calling me to his office to tell me what had happened. It was, he said, a serious breach of discipline, and he was going to recommend to the board that all four were sacked. I think he felt that was the only way out of the situation. It was a very difficult position for him. Bobby Moore was one of the greatest players in the world at the time and was captain of both England and West Ham. But Ron believed that what he intended to do was the right course of action for the club. As a manager, you have to evaluate incidents like that carefully, but once they reach the newspapers they develop a fresh momentum and there is a danger of getting the whole thing out of perspective. Ron had made up his mind, though, and at the next board meeting he recommended that all four players be dismissed.

Mr Pratt didn't agree. He was his own man. He wanted to keep them – at least for the time being. All four stayed with the club, though Bobby was stripped of the captaincy.

That incident, I think, illustrated Mr Pratt's independence, though 99 times out of 100 he and his board backed the manager to the hilt. I was to learn, however, that occasionally the board would overrule the manager's proposals concerning new players. It was because of him the club paid a world-record transfer fee for a goalkeeper – Phil Parkes of Queen's Park Rangers. It was February 1979 and I was manager. I felt a goalkeeper of his quality would give us the little bit of extra impetus to get us back into the First Division. I've always felt that if a special goalkeeper could save you ten goals a season it could be the difference between success and failure. I had been looking for a new goalkeeper for four or five months. Mervyn Day was West Ham's first-choice goalkeeper at the time and, as a teenager, had been truly outstanding. He was only 18 when he was selected for the England Under-23 team and he appeared to have a wonderful career ahead of him. Everything was going well for him, but suddenly he stopped performing as I knew he could. He was an honest lad and a hard worker, but I think he lost confidence. It happens to a lot of young goalkeepers. The problem is that a goalkeeper is so exposed in his role that if he loses confidence it tends to seep through to the rest of the team. Maybe his nature was such that he needed to move clubs to find the right environment. I'm delighted to say that he has since proved to be a good and consistently reliable goalkeeper with Leyton Orient, Aston Villa and Leeds United.

It is not a problem exclusively confined to goalkeepers. Trevor Brooking had a similar loss of confidence in his early days at West Ham. But Trevor won his personal battles with himself and played his way through it. But at one time it was a serious problem and Ron Greenwood was intending to sell him.

It was Mervyn's lack of confidence that made me feel we needed another goalkeeper, and Eddie Baily and I tracked Phil Parkes for four or five months. Finally, we reached a situation where I felt we had a chance of buying him. Queen's Park Rangers wanted £475,000 for him, but with the tax and other bits and pieces the club would have to invest £565,000. It was an enormous outlay for a Second Division club at that time. I went to the board and told them that I wanted to buy Phil Parkes and he would cost us a fortune. I told them that I felt such a good goalkeeper was worth the investment. We discussed the implications for two hours. There were four directors of the club at the time – Mr Pratt, the chairman, and the three Cearns brothers, Mr Len, Mr Will and Brian. Mr Pratt called for a vote. The four of them voted and they were split, two for and two against. We all looked at Mr Pratt who, as chairman, had a casting vote. There was a long silence. Mr Pratt rose quietly from the table, went behind his high-backed chair, put on his coat and picked up his briefcase. He stood behind the chair with his hands on the back.

'Gentlemen,' he said. 'Two things are going to happen. The first thing is that I am going home to have tea with my wife. The second thing is that John is going to buy Phil Parkes.'

He departed. The rest of us sat there looking at each other, wondering whether he would come back, poke his head round the door and say: 'I'm joking, of course.' He didn't do that. A few days later I bought Phil Parkes, and he proved to be one of the best signings of my career.

Mr Pratt retired as chairman in 1979, and although sadly no longer with us, I have never forgotten his advice, his caring nature and his understated sense of humour. Not long before he retired I was due to take the players and their wives to a Christmas cabaret but, because of transfer business, had to suddenly pull out of the function. I called Mr Pratt to explain the situation, and he said he would willingly go the cabaret with the players and act as host. A couple of days later I called him at his home in Wanstead.

'How did you enjoy the cabaret, Mr Pratt?' I asked.

'Pardon?' he replied.

I repeated my question. 'How did you enjoy the cabaret, Mr Pratt?'

'Pardon?'

'Mr Pratt, what's the problem?'

'John,' he said, 'I'm still deaf from sitting next to the loudspeakers at that cabaret.'

When Mr Pratt retired as chairman, Mr Len took over. As you would expect, nothing changed apart from the personnel. Mr Len, the current chairman, was steeped in West Ham's traditions, and he, too, wanted to ensure their continuity. He is an upright, conservative English gentleman, acutely aware of his responsibilities, not just to the club, but to the supporters and shareholders. Even when Mr Pratt was chairman, Mr Len helped control the club's finances. He ensured there was no wastage. He is a very efficient man and ensures that the finances of the club are in good order. He is also an expert on rules and regulations, both in the accountancy field and in football generally. In recent years he has taken a great interest in the introduction of synthetic pitches. I remember him asking me: 'Why have we got them, John? Who benefits?' He has never courted publicity, but has made a tremendous contribution to the game, in my opinion. I would have to say of both Mr Len and Mr Pratt that, over their years of service, they gave far more to the game than they ever took from it.

Mr Len is the middle of the three Cearns brothers who served on the board. The oldest is Mr Will – and I always addressed him in the same way as Mr Len. Mr Will is a marvellous man, a real extrovert. He is a retired solicitor, who for a long time did a lot of legal work for the club. He's always bright and jolly and enjoys football, but it is not the be-all and end-all of his life. He particularly enjoyed the tours abroad and the European ties when West Ham were involved on foreign fields. Football people tend to avoid the tourist traps, but if the offer of a sightseeing tour came along, Mr Will would be the first with his hand up. On tours he usually travelled with his younger brother Brian. It was my job when we were abroad to control the finances, and I would give them their daily spending money just as if they were players. They wanted to be treated like everyone else.

Of the three brothers, I was probably closest to Brian Cearns. Apart from anything else, he was closer to my own age and he was football mad. I think he would have enjoyed the life of a football manager. Like me, he felt that any money the club had should be spent on buying players, if necessary. If I wanted to spend £1 million he'd say: 'Let's do it. We're only here once.' He was my sort of man. Of course, you need a balance on a board of directors, and Mr Len provided that. Brian became a great ally to me within the club. We would often sit together on the team coach travelling home from away matches. Having got the emotion of the game over, we would talk about the club. He would ask: 'Is there anything you need, John?'

I remember telling him once that I felt the club as a whole – players, supporters and local community – would benefit enormously from a well-equipped gymnasium at our Chadwell Heath training headquarters. At the next board meeting he remarked to the chairman: 'We ought to be thinking about building a gym at Chadwell Heath.' Eventually we had a superb gym built at a cost of £140,000 with £100,000 coming from a Sports Council grant that I helped to negotiate. Brian would invariably see the football man's point of view. I could drop a hint, knowing that the chances were that he would follow it up with the board. He was a good friend to both Ron Greenwood and myself.

Brian was a stout character, a director of a number of companies and a captain in the Sixth Airborne Division during the war. He joined his brothers on the board in 1962. Sadly he developed a serious illness later in his life, but I never once heard him complain. He once underwent three major operations in a week, made a good recovery and came back to see us at the club. I was very upset when he finally lost his battle.

From 1948 until the present day, at least one of the three brothers – there were four Cearns brothers in all – served on the board. In 1978 a new generation, the fourth generation of Cearns, joined the board. Martin, son of Mr Len, works in banking and is a possible future chairman. He, and another newcomer to the board, Jack Petchey, joined the club at a time of change among the great dynasties in the First Division. Personally, I would also have liked to see a man of stature and football achievement – Ron Greenwood is the perfect example – on the board. This would have given that fine balance between football and finance that is so difficult to attain. The day of the businessman running his local club as a hobby was coming to an end. We were now entering the era of the high-profile, big-business impressario – Robert Maxwell, Ken Bates, Irving Scholar, Elton John, Sam Hammam, Ron Noades and, most recently Michael Knighton, the man who tried to buy Manchester United for £20 million.

Nothing is forever, and football isn't exempt from that rule. The sport has to evolve, to keep pace with the changes in society. There have been many big takeovers of the major clubs and many of the clubs have benefited enormously from new, progressive leadership. Irving Scholar, the chairman of Tottenham, is a good example. A successful businessman, he was steeped in Tottenham tradition long before he became chairman. He has made many changes at the club, but I think he has always had the good of the club and the game at heart. And, despite what some say, he has not always made decisions purely for financial reasons. Football is a strange business, with a financial structure that probably applies to no other business. A manager can spend £100,000 on a player many people don't think is very good, and sell him two years later for £2 million. Equally, he can spend £2 million on a player everyone thinks is brilliant and two years later struggle to get £100,000 for him. It is an area where there is no black and white, no hard-and-fast rules. I have no doubt that the financial risks are becoming greater in today's game, and that is putting increased pressure on boardrooms throughout the Football League.

Stability, in my opinion, therefore remains an integral part of a successful club. Liverpool and Arsenal, the latter a club of family traditions much like West Ham, remain prime examples of that. I think there is still room for a club with West Ham's values and standards in today's game. There has to be, because clubs like West Ham give the game stability. The high-profile impresarios might monopolize the publicity, but if you visited, say, Liverpool and Crewe you would probably find both clubs adopting a similar set of values. Crewe, who have made significant progress under manager Dario Gradi, probably have a board of directors who plough their own money into the club, devote their time to it, watch the team and get a bit of fun out of their commitment. Those people are doing a good service for the sport – and there are hundreds like them in football. We tend to disregard the good they do and concentrate instead on the publicity seekers.

I am a traditionalist, but I accept that every board of directors needs a balance. I think we had that balance at West Ham. Some might feel that the club's standards and tradition hampered our efforts to win the First Division title. I never felt that. I never wanted to let anyone down. The board gave me tremendous help and I felt I owed them a debt. When I was manager at West Ham we wanted to play the game well and entertain the fans. We could have played a different style and still not won the Championship – many teams go down the same route season after season. The only way I could have had it better as manager, and West Ham could have had more chance of winning the title, is if we had millions of pounds to spend on players. But that wasn't realistic. That's dreaming.

Throughout my time as manager we always balanced the books to the satisfaction of the board. We didn't borrow money, and the board's careful housekeeping ensured that we were never seriously in debt. It was our policy to keep transfer spending within the club's financial resources. If we made a handsome profit, as we did in the FA Cup Final year of 1980, we had the money to buy top-class players. The example that year was Paul Goddard, who cost £800,000 from Queen's Park Rangers. I had to accept, of course, that if the club only broke even, the money available for transfers was greatly reduced. Of course, in recent seasons, outgoing transfers have produced enormous revenue, and when I left Upton Park the club had at least £2 million in the bank.

Every club changes, and West Ham is no exception. I think Martin Cearns will protect the traditions he has inherited from his father and uncles – if he has the chance. If he becomes chairman he will have to do as I did, and establish his authority quickly. It is never an easy situation. Jack Petchey is not in the mould of a traditional West Ham director. He is a highly successful businessman with an enquiring mind, the sort of man who will sit and talk to you for hours, make notes and then follow everything up thoroughly. When West Ham play away he makes a point of walking around the host club to see how they do things.

He's from Manor Park and served in the Fleet Air Arm before embarking on a business career with garages, car-hire firms and property investment at home and abroad. He was a long-time season-ticket holder and an avid West Ham fan long before he joined the board. He can be pleasant, but behind the smile he can be a ruthless man too. He is very ambitious for the club, and if a difficult decision had to be made, he would not hesitate to make it if he felt it was for the good of the club.

He was an opportunist. We often shared a chuckle round the boardroom table, because we knew that when the chairman enquired wearily: 'Any other business, gentlemen?' Jack would invariably put forward his proposal. His interest at the club was largely commercial, and if, for instance, he felt he needed some cash to advertise a new promotion, he wouldn't raise the matter in the commercial report, but wait for any other business!

When I left the club the fifth member of the board was Charles Warner, who had been such a short time at Upton Park that I barely got to know him. He is, significantly, the family solicitor and a relation of the Hills, the descendants of the club's founder and still the major shareholders. The Hills' influence on the club's destiny was restored when he joined the board.

These were the five men who decided between them to not renew my contract. With the exception of Mr Warner, I knew them all well and had a good working relationship with them all. I never sensed any resentment from any of the board. My misfortune as a player had taken me into all the areas of the club, so I knew how the club operated, from top to bottom. Above and beyond that, I had a wonderful teacher in Ron Greenwood and I knew how to manage all aspects of the club. If I was asked for an opinion I would give it. Sometimes they were strong opinions. Most of the time the board would accept without question what I said about football policy. They never interfered with football matters and I don't recall one serious argument with any of them. When they came to sack me the voting was split. I still don't know who wanted me out and who wanted me to stay — maybe I never will.

Nothing has changed my opinion of the club, though, and I hope that when Mr Len retires and a new chairman takes over he cherishes the traditions of West Ham and tries to add to them. The club is an institution and it is worth preserving. It gives the local people a sense of identity, and they have responded over the years with their loyalty. It's hard to measure the loyalty of supporters, but I can't think of another club that has established a greater rapport with the local community. I have never forgotten what Derek Hales said to me after making his debut against Middlesbrough at Upton Park in October 1977. We lost 2–0, but we were applauded off the pitch by the fans. Hales sat in the dressing room afterwards, scratching his head. 'I can't believe those fans, John,' he said. 'At other clubs, when you lose at home you sprint down the tunnel at the final whistle.'

I personally owe a great debt to the West Ham fans who showed such loyalty to me and the team over the years. A lot of the families who traditionally followed West Ham have long since left the East End of London, but fathers and sons still travel from all over the south of England to Upton Park on match days. After my dismissal I had dozens of letters from West Ham supporters from all over the country — Gloucester, Liverpool, Newcastle, Southampton. I was quite touched, too, by the show of loyalty from the terraces after our final home game of last season. We beat Luton 1–0 and were still in peril at the bottom of the First Division, but at the end of the match they chanted 'Johnny Lyall's claret and blue army' as though we had just won the title. I was so sorry to disappoint them. East Londoners tend to be family people and, for me, those supporters were all part of the West Ham family.

The best memories, of course, concern the days immediately after our two FA Cup Final wins in 1975 and 1980. It was worth getting to Wembley just to share the joy of the local people. I often wonder how they would react if West Ham were to win the First Division title. The crowds that greeted us on our return to East Ham after beating Arsenal in 1980 were awesome, so dense in fact that the double-decker bus taking us to the town hall was frequently halted. It was a glorious, warm day, and mounted policemen had to edge through the crowds in the streets to clear a path for the bus. The fans were hanging out of the windows in tower blocks and sending jugs of beer out of the pubs for the players, who were quite moved by the emotion of it all. At one stage the bus was halted by the crowds immediately outside a massage and sauna parlour. A man, who I guess was the owner, and two scantily clad girls, were leaning out of an upstairs window waving at the players. The man shouted at me: 'Tell the boys, John, any time they want to come along – and it won't cost them a penny!' A kind offer, I thought, but I didn't mention it to the lads.

It was from this great mass of people in east London that the club traditionally drew most of its playing staff. Although the movement of the population is now changing that – some families who have lived for generations in the area are now moving further into the suburbs and the Home Counties – it is easy to understand why the club has such a close affinity with the local inhabitants. When I was a young coach at West Ham, all the other coaches, Jimmy Barrett, who gave me many tips in my early days, Albert Walker and Ernie

Gregory, were former players. Albert first joined the club as a player in 1932 and had completed nearly fifty years of service at Upton Park before retiring. Originally a left back, like me, he enjoyed a long and distinguished playing career before joining the coaching staff, finally becoming one of our invaluable backroom boys. Ron Greenwood made him team attendant towards the end of his time at Upton Park, simply because the club were travelling with so much kit that it was a job that could no longer be looked after on a part-time basis by the physiotherapist. Like everything else, Albert fulfilled that duty diligently. After every training session that I took, Albert always provided me with a clean towel and a new piece of soap – every session, every day.

During the work we did at our training headquarters at Chadwell Heath, Ron and I both tried to instil a sense of team spirit, not just in the senior players, but in everyone connected with the club. I have always believed that everyone benefits if we all pull together. Two summers ago, myself, the coaching staff and all the YTS kids at the club painted the pavilion at the training ground. Every year the club gives a Christmas party there for the players and their families. Each family receives a turkey, all the children get a really nice present, and the backroom staff all get one week's wages. It's been that way for as long as I have been with West Ham.

The coaching staff I left behind – an excellent bunch of men – all fell into the traditional West Ham mould. Ronnie Boyce, Mick McGiven, Tony Carr, Ernie Gregory and Billy Bonds were all players with the club. Just as important to me in his role as physiotherapist was Rob Jenkins, who succeeded his father in 1966. Ronnie Boyce is a marvellous lad, very sensible and mature and a deep thinker about the game. He is an easy fellow to talk to, and a lot of the players like to have a quiet chat with him about the game. He was, of course, a great player in his own right. He came from East Ham, joined the club as a groundstaff boy in 1959 and finally retired after a wonderful career in 1972. I'd put him in my list of all-time great players at West Ham. He was a superb interceptor and a good and intelligent passer of the ball. He was a thoughtful player, listening to all he was told and learning from it. We called him 'Ticker' in his playing days, because when he was ticking over well the whole team seemed to play well. As a player he epitomized all the good things Ron Greenwood stood for as a manager. Even now, when he plays in the gym with the youngsters, his touch is sure and his technique is excellent. I've seen some of the young kids looking at him in awe.

He shared the first-team coaching duties along with Mick McGiven, who is a completely different type. He comes from Newcastle upon Tyne and is a volatile, demanding type of coach. He played for Sunderland as a half back and joined West Ham in 1973. His career at Upton Park was dogged by injuries – I remember him losing four teeth in a clash with Liverpool's Phil Thompson – and eventually he was forced to hang up his boots. He was a committed player and is the same as a coach. He usually finished each game with his voice hoarse from shouting at the players. You can usually hear him from every corner of Upton Park. He's very different from Ronnie, but together they provide a good balance.

Tony Carr was a quite outstanding youth player. He was a centre forward, and captained the East London Boys team that won the English Schools Trophy in 1966. He was in one of my youth groups but didn't quite make the grade, and instead became the sports master at Holloway School. He coached at West Ham for seven years on a part-time basis, and I eventually appointed him youth team coach in 1980. When I left he was reserve team manager.

By then I had given the job of youth team coach to Billy Bonds, who would also be in my list of all-time great players at West Ham. I think he is still going through the learning process as a coach at the moment, but I'm confident that he'll do well. I think he was amazed at the amount of work coaching involved. Working with young players is not easy, because they are so inconsistent. They don't always grasp what you are telling them immediately and you have to be patient. Bill's first year as coach wasn't helped by an appalling list of injuries. He often had to field nine schoolboys in his youth team, but by the end of the season I think he was beginning to enjoy it. He impressed me greatly because he has taken the same qualities into coaching that he had as a player.

Like so many before him at Upton Park, Ernie Gregory achieved almost legendary status. When he retired he was the longest-serving member of the West Ham staff and had become a kindly grandfather figure to the rest of the 'family'. He came from Stratford and first caught the eye of Charlie Paynter in 1936, when he played for the West Ham Boys team against Preston in the English Trophy Final. He played for the amateurs of Leytonstone, helping them win the old Isthmian League Championship, before signing professional forms with West Ham in 1939. His war service in the Essex Regiment interrupted his football career, but in 1946 he was given the goalkeeper's first-team jersey at West Ham and wore it with pride and distinction until 1959. He played nearly 500 games for West Ham, won an England 'B' cap, and was awarded the Football League's Long Service Statuette.

He has been a good, honest friend to me, full of solid advice and ideas. In his later years at the club he used to assess the strengths and weaknesses of opponents for me – and did an invaluable job. Equally as important was his daily training of our goalkeepers. Mention Ernie to Phil Parkes and he would sing his praises for hours. Ernie remains a West Ham man through and through, much loved at Upton Park.

Players like Parkes have great respect for him because Ernie, of course, went through the treadmill in the days before law changes and stricter refereeing made goalkeeping a less hazardous occupation. Ernie still loves to recall the battles and scrapes he had in his playing career – and he has the scars to prove it.

The last, and certainly one of the most vital, members of my branch of the West Ham family was Eddie Baily, who, if not a familiar face to the terrace fan, is one of the best-known personalities within the game. Eddie was my chief scout and, as such, had a crucial role to play in unearthing young talent and signing experienced players from other clubs. I have known him for years, and he has become one of the best-loved characters on the London soccer scene. He was a very good inside forward in Arthur Rowe's 'push and run' Tottenham team that won the Second Division Championship in 1950 and the First Division Championship in 1951. The fact that he was capped nine times by England illustrates his worth as a player in those days. After leaving Spurs, he played for Port Vale and Nottingham Forest and returned to London as a player-coach with Leyton Orient. He went back

to White Hart Lane as a coaching assistant to manager Bill
Nicholson, who eventually became one of the all-time greats
of soccer management, and between them they won the
League and FA Cup 'double' in 1961 and enjoyed great
success in the early days of the European competitions. When
Bill resigned at Spurs, Eddie went too. He worked in local
schools, and grew increasingly disillusioned with the professional game. Bill Nicholson later worked with Ron Greenwood and me at Upton Park for a year, and when he
returned to Spurs to work for Keith Burkinshaw, their new
manager, Ron suggested we replace him with Eddie, the
ideal successor. He joined us in 1976, and immediately his
forthright opinions and humour were filtering through the
club. Eddie has been great company to me over the years –
he is honest and efficient, and his administration work is
superb. I never played against him but I can imagine that he
was a formidable opponent. I remember him goading armed
Soviet soldiers during a snowbound stopover at Moscow
airport – we were on our way to play in Tbilisi – because
they refused to allow him to use the toilet. He soon made
them realize the error of their ways.

These are the people Lou Macari has had the good fortune
to inherit. They are good people with good standards. They
didn't ever let me down, and they won't let him down. We
had our highs and lows, like most clubs, but for the thirty-
four years I was there West Ham served the professional
game well and enhanced the good things in the sport. I have
spoken to Lou since he took charge, and I wished him every
success. I am sure that in time he, like myself, Ron and Ted
before him, will feel gratitude to the local people who
support the club.

He has inherited a lot of good things, and I hope he protects those things as he takes the club into a new era. I hope he benefits from the traditions of a family club – a club that unites to help out the victims of misfortune. All victims, whether they are 23, like I was with a shattered knee, or unknown apprentices like Gerhardt Ampofo, who spent two years in and out of hospital after a terrible compound fracture of a leg. He was a promising player who never got into the first team, and now never will. The club organized a testimonial game for him against Tottenham and raised £7,000.

Perhaps the people Lou will come to appreciate most are the West Ham supporters. The day after I left the club, a young man I'd never previously met, Chris Reeve, a West Ham fan from childhood, arrived at the Chadwell Heath training ground and announced to Billy Bonds that he wanted to buy me a farewell gift.

A few days later Mick McGiven drove Chris to my house. He presented Yvonne with a beautiful display of silk flowers, and gave me a fishing reel and a £50 voucher for fishing equipment.

West Ham fans are special people.

THE GREENWOOD INFLUENCE

Probably the most exciting and stimulating period of my career were the years I spent learning the basics of coaching from Ron Greenwood. He was a constant source of inspiration to me. I had not set out to be a coach; when my playing career was prematurely ended by injury I went into coaching with little practical experience and even less knowledge. But suddenly, under Ron's wing, I discovered that I couldn't learn enough. I had a completely open mind on coaching and I devoured everything he said. I could listen to him talking about the game for hours. He created pictures of situations for his players. He told me that every time I took a training session I should do likewise – create the picture that helped the players understand what was required.

I had done some coaching, but mostly with youths and amateurs. When I was about 17, John Cunningham, the schoolteacher who had recommended me to West Ham as a player, told me that a local team called Ilford Youth were looking for a coach. They were lads in the 16–18 age group. I used to coach them at Fairlop School one evening a week. Another team called Hampshire Sports, a very useful side in local football, used to follow them into the gym for their training session, and they eventually asked me to coach them too. That was a particularly good experience for me, because with Hampshire Sports I was dealing with men. I was only a youngster but I never felt intimidated by them. They were simply keen to learn. All I did in those days was imitate the training routines we used at West Ham. But it was sometimes frustrating trying to coach players of a lower level to achieve the skills and fitness of the professionals at Upton Park. It was a lesson for me, and I soon realized that I had to tailor my coaching sessions to the level of the players I was dealing with.

I remember a graphic example of this when I was about 23, a time when my playing career was in the balance because of my knee injury. At the time I was coaching Old Parkonians, my school's old-boys team. For the first few weeks in pre-season I gave them some light running, but concentrated on skills, and the response was reasonable. But, as the season approached, I decided to give them some heavy running, and after the first session most of them were ill. What is so typical of footballers at this level, however, is that when we had finished they all stood and applauded me, and those that were still able to said: 'That was great, John, a great session. We really enjoyed it.' I realized then that to get the best out of players during a coaching session, it helps if they enjoy it. I remember one chap, though, a schoolteacher who used to arrive by bike, asking me how concerned I was about the injury that now threatened my playing career. 'I bet you now wish you'd stayed at school,' he said. I pointed out to him, as he climbed on to his bike, that while my short career as a player might be over, it had provided me with a house in Abridge and a nice little car. He cycled off without another word.

That, then, was practically the full extent of my coaching experience when I started working with the youth players at

West Ham. Ron and his other coaches were enormously supportive, and the youngsters they had at West Ham wanted to learn and wanted to impress.

I began to pick up the phrases Ron used daily in his coaching sessions. They have stuck with me all my life. One of the earliest, and truest, was 'Simplicity is genius'. I was beginning to realize that the best football, like that played by the modern-day Liverpool team, is the simplest. That phrase became one of the rocks upon which I built my own coaching reputation. I like good players who do simple things well.

Ron also liked players with 'good habits'. This didn't mean that they held a teacup with the correct degree of finesse, though he admired good behaviour and good manners in his players. He meant that players who consistently do the right things on the playing field develop good habits and become good players. Those with bad habits, he would argue, become inconsistent players. Yet he also felt that one of the most important arts of the game was the ability to improvise, the ability to surprise the opposition with the unpredictable. The complete footballer was the one who could combine good habits with improvisation.

He used to tell all his players: 'You must leave the ball playable.' This meant that when making a pass the receiving player had to be able to play the ball first time. This was a good habit. If the pass was perfect, the receiving player could play the ball, spin away from his marker and move into space to collect a return. This was improvisation. This was what he taught at West Ham, and it was a joy to watch him at work with players of the quality of Bobby Moore, Martin Peters, Geoff Hurst, Johnny Byrne and Ronnie Boyce.

As a player with an enquiring mind, Ron had been enormously impressed by the wonderful Hungarian side that beat England 6–3 at Wembley in 1953. It was a historic defeat, the first England had suffered at Wembley against a foreign team. That Hungarian triumph proved to him that football could be a game of beauty and art, as well as a muscular science. He once said that he came away from Wembley that day with a little insight into how Paul must have felt on the road to Damascus. He applied many of the features he saw in that Hungarian side to his own West Ham teams over the years. One tactic used by the Hungarians in later years also had a big influence on Ron, and he was to use it with enormous success at West Ham.

He had recognized the value of the near-post cross used by the Hungarians, and embedded that tactic into the framework of West Ham's attacking game. The near-post cross, an innovation in the English game, became a Greenwood speciality. The essence of the move was that the ball was whipped in quickly from the flanks to unmarked space at the near post. The key to the move was that the central strikers anticipated the flight and timing of the cross and ran into the empty space as late as possible to head or volley the ball towards the goal. He first developed this move with Martin Peters, Peter Brabrook, Johnny Sissons and Geoff Hurst, with Bobby Moore also involved as the player feeding an early pass out to the flanks. The delivery of the ball into the penalty area had to be perfect but, equally important, Hurst, as the main central striker, had to get the timing of his runs to the near post exactly right. I remember spending months and months on the training pitches at Chadwell Heath perfecting the tactic. Ron had the training-ground maintenance staff stick a couple of posts in two huge paint tins filled with concrete. These posts were positioned out on the flanks and acted as markers. The wide players, Sissons and Peters (and, later, Harry Redknapp and Johnny Ayris – Ron insisted that all players at all levels learned the move), had to run at the paint tins, pretending they were markers. The players then had to push the ball outside the tins but, before they went beyond them, had to curl their cross round the tins to the near post. The central strikers would start their runs from the far side of the penalty area. They had to leave the space at the near post empty for as long as they could, otherwise the defenders would follow them and the element of surprise was lost. Hurst, for instance, perfected his dummy run at this time, lingering on the edge of the area before making a decoy run. The marking defender would follow him, and Hurst would suddenly change direction and sprint into the space at the near post, arriving just in time to meet the ball from the wing.

That move brought West Ham literally dozens of goals over the years and, inevitably, was widely copied by other teams. Perhaps the most memorable example of Hurst's near-post expertise came at Wembley in 1966, not in West Ham's claret and blue, but in England's red shirts. England were trailing 1–0 to West Germany, when Overath fouled Bobby Moore. The England captain took the West German defence completely by surprise with a quick, long and accurate free kick from out on the left. Hurst, almost programmed by now to expect such a ball to the near post, timed his run from the right immaculately, gliding the ball with his head past Tilkowski. It was a goal that had its origins on the training ground at Chadwell Heath. It was as if the relationship that day between the three West Ham lads, Hurst,

Moore and Peters, was telepathic. Ron put it more simply. It was good habits.

The longer I worked with him, the more I realized that one of his greatest strengths was his ability to spot the central problems every time. He would sit the players in the dressing room and say, in quite straightforward terms, that this is where we were at fault and this is what we had to do to rectify the problem. There were times when he could be dogmatic, but I think a good coach has to be like that. But he would always put his ideas across in an intelligent and creative manner. If you had any football brain at all he was easy to understand. You have only to look at the number of his players who went on to become internationals, and then coaches and managers themselves, to realize that the vast majority of them learned a great deal from Ron Greenwood.

He taught them, too, about life and how, as public figures, they should behave and handle themselves. He taught me always to talk to the people who guide you to the car park, open the door for you or give you your match programme. He believed in respect and good manners. He was a kind, caring and thoroughly decent man who loved his job – and football – in all its aspects.

He had an encyclopaedic knowledge of world football, all the coaches and all the major players. We could be in, say, Amsterdam, and I would sit alongside him at a match, enthralled as he pointed out the strengths and weaknesses of teams and individuals. 'Do you see what they're doing there, John?' he would ask me. I learned a tremendous amount from our trips to watch foreign games, and there is still a great deal I admire about Continental football. The modern-day Liverpool team have woven many of the finest European techniques into their game. Their art, just as Ron used to preach, is keeping the game simple. Many teams and players are sometimes not satisfied with the simple things. They don't appreciate that it is the best way, they over-complicate the game. But Liverpool have kept their game simple, and have thus set the standard for the rest of us in the Football League. They have combined traditional British qualities with the simplicity, individuality and technique of the European game. If UEFA, the ruling body of football in Europe, lifted the ban on English clubs, I believe Liverpool would still be the team every club on the Continent would want to beat.

Liverpool do the simple things well. It is the corner-stone of their coaching philosophy. But I have learned that it is human nature that some players are not satisfied with the simple things, and always want to do a little bit extra. Most players in this category tend to overstretch themselves, but as a coach you are sometimes thankful for the few with a unique talent. As a player, Trevor Brooking came into this category at West Ham. If I wanted to demonstrate a simple move in training I would often use Trevor. Of course, he could do it the way I wanted, but he could also do it his own way, and often twice as efficiently. If I asked him to lay off the ball with the inside of his foot he might, instead, lay it off with the outside of the other foot.

It was all a bit tongue in cheek on his part. He knew exactly what I wanted, but he knew, too, that he was good enough to improvise. I remember scratching my head on more than one occasion and asking myself: 'Why have I got *him* to demonstrate? What have I done?'

Trevor had been one of the first players I worked with in my youth squad at Upton Park, and by the time Ron

JUST LIKE MY DREAMS

appointed me assistant manager in 1971 he was, of course, a well-established first-team man. My apprenticeship as a coach could not have been any more comprehensive. I had been involved in most aspects of coaching and Ron had even sent me to lecture a group of London coaches at Baker Street in London on Monday evenings. This wasn't a question of coaching professional footballers. It was a matter of teaching people from all walks of life to be football coaches. 'If you want to be a coach you have to learn to teach properly,' Ron told me. It was a good experience because I would get a bank manager, a railway clerk or a hotel porter asking me the sort of questions I had rarely faced before.

I was also well versed in the art of assessing opponents and players. I will always remember my debut as a soccer scout for West Ham, though not because of the football. It took place on a wet winter's evening at Ipswich. It had poured with rain all day, and Yvonne insisted I take my new umbrella with me. I arrived at Portman Road three hours before the match, parked my car, and decided to walk into the town to find a restaurant. As I walked through Ipswich, huddled under my new umbrella, I realized that my priorities were changing: I needed to visit the toilet before finding a restaurant. Eventually, in an unlit side-street, I found a toilet, but the entrance was too narrow for the umbrella. I tried to close the umbrella, but couldn't. Nor could I leave it outside in the street because the wind would carry it half way across Suffolk.

In my desperation I wrestled with the stays of the umbrella for several minutes, but they wouldn't budge. I put the umbrella on the ground, looked up and down the street to ensure that no one was about, and then jumped on it and

72

crunched it up as small as I could get it. I strode triumphantly into the toilet, deposited the umbrella in a corner, and, as I was opening the front of my raincoat, noticed blood gushing from my hands. In trying to force the stays of the umbrella shut I had cut the fingers on both hands. Even so, the sense of relief was enormous, but I sat through dinner and, later, the match, wringing wet with my hands swathed in handkerchiefs. A memorable evening!

Ron's tutorship helped me pass the Football Association's preliminary coaching badge at 20 and the full badge four years later. By the time I became assistant manager, I felt confident and capable of working with senior professional players. Of course, many of them were former playing colleagues of a similar age. I was determined to succeed with them, and I happily accepted the responsibility Ron had given me. But I knew I would have to work to gain the respect of the players. I felt if I was fair and honest with them they would appreciate my efforts as a coach. I was critical of them at times but, as a group, they never took umbrage and were, in fact, a great help to me. If I criticized them, they accepted it and got on with the job. On my first day at Chadwell Heath I remember getting a rather casual response from one or two of the players when I blew the whistle to start training. I can remember at that moment recalling an incident during a coaching session at Stepney Green School, when a master's whistle had brought a similar response. I did exactly what the schoolteacher had done that day. I told the players to wander off into the far corners of the field but next time, when I blew the whistle, I wanted a far crisper response . . . from everyone. Fortunately, I got it. I had made my first point.

For me it was a privilege to work with so many talented players and enjoy the benefits of Ron's wisdom. One evening we were sitting in his car outside Upton Park discussing players – sometimes we'd do this until two in the morning after a match – when he told me that he wanted me to take sole charge of the first team for the next game. The match was against Manchester City at Upton Park in February 1971, and that Saturday Ron was making a secret trip to St James' Park to watch the Newcastle striker Bryan Robson. We drew my first match in charge 0–0, but perhaps more significant was Ron's enthusiasm when he returned from Newcastle.

'I've seen an outstanding player,' he told me. 'He does everything I would have liked to coach into a player, but he does it naturally. He would be a wonderful acquisition for us.' A few days later, 'Pop' Robson signed for West Ham from Newcastle for £120,000. On his first day at training, Ron asked me to show him a few routines and explain to him why we did certain things during the course of a game. It immediately struck me that everything Ron had told me about Pop was absolutely correct. Ron had summed up his strengths perfectly. Pop was a super player, and he even made those late runs to the near post, a facet of his game that would have appealed enormously to Ron. Pop became a prolific goalscorer during his two spells at West Ham, and we established a firm friendship that survives to this day.

I was sorry to see him go when he joined Sunderland. He wanted to return to his native north-east for family reasons. But he loved London, and particularly West Ham, and when he heard that we wanted him back at Upton Park he jumped at the chance to renew old friendships. He even bought back the house he had previously owned in Woodford Green.

The game was buoyant during that period of the early seventies, and although Sir Alf Ramsey's England team had lost the World Cup in Mexico in 1970 the nation's football reputation was still high. The crowds flocked through the turnstiles – nearly 29 million in 1971–2 compared to 18 million in 1988–9 – and the First Division was full of glamorous names like George Best, Bobby Charlton, Denis Law, Gordon Banks, Francis Lee, Rodney Marsh, Alan Ball, Billy Bremner, Martin Chivers and, of course, Hurst, Moore and Peters. I grew to appreciate entertaining sides, but I was also becoming aware that there wasn't just one way to play the game. I admired all kinds of teams for different reasons, and still do. I came to realize that a coach has to maximize the strengths of the players at his disposal. If you have good ball players, you can play an entertaining type of game. If you don't have good ball players, you have to play a more functional game. Not all footballers are outstandingly talented as individuals, so a coach inevitably has to weld them into a disciplined framework.

My personal preference is for the teams that attack with style and give the fans some entertainment value. I particularly enjoyed watching Tommy Docherty's Manchester United team evolve in the mid seventies. I admired the way he pinned his hopes on the two wingers, Steve Coppell and Gordon Hill. They were a good team to watch, and when they had a front four of Stuart Pearson, Jimmy Greenhoff, Coppell and Hill they were probably the most powerful attacking team in the country. Tottenham, too, have had some very entertaining teams over the years, and I also had a high regard for Bertie Mee's Arsenal team that won the fabled League and FA Cup 'double' in 1971. Don Howe's coaching ensured they were well organized, and as a fellow coach, if a much junior one, I thought that Don and Bertie had created a super team at Highbury.

One of the most interesting aspects of the Football League – and in a way one of its great strengths – is that so many teams play contrasting styles. It's not easy for the players or the coaches because, most weeks, they have to adjust their pattern of play to some degree to cater for the opposition. If you think that the opposition can overcome your style, you have to find a way of playing that can still counteract them.

All these contrasting styles, of course, present the England manager Bobby Robson with innumerable problems. I believe that there has to be room in the League for all styles of play; there is no system that is perfect, because every system can be overcome if you have players of sufficient quality. That is the constant challenge of the game. But for Bobby, it's a constant headache. The club sides in many Continental countries share a common style – and the national team manager benefits. If the West German manager, Franz Beckenbauer, wants a right back he looks at all the teams in the Bundesliga and selects the best right back purely on merit. He knows that player will be well versed in the system his team adopts. It is more complicated for Bobby, because the right back he wants may be used to a system that he doesn't intend employing. And sometimes he has no more than one or two training sessions before a big game to help integrate a new player. His players, used to operating in different styles and formations at club level, must suddenly blend as a team unit. A coach needs longer than two training sessions to get that blend right, in my opinion.

Bobby was a very successful club manager at Ipswich, and

it was very satisfying for me when West Ham beat his team in the FA Cup semifinal in 1975. Many of his players had come through the Portman Road Youth scheme. It must have taken a tremendous effort to put that team together, because at the smaller clubs you have to pit yourself against the giants of the game, and that is never easy. He lost several top-class players to bigger clubs – Paul Mariner and Brian Talbot to Arsenal and Alan Brazil to Tottenham. But one of the saddest moments of Bobby's career must have been the loss of Kevin Beattie, an awesomely powerful defender who could have been one of the game's all-time greats. He retired prematurely through injury.

I felt for Beattie, having suffered a similar experience. As a player he combined strength with style and epitomized the qualities of Bobby's teams at Ipswich. They were always effective and always entertaining; then Bobby added a further ingredient when he went to Holland to sign Arnold Muhren and Frans Thijssen, two outstandingly talented Dutch internationals. With them in their team, Ipswich had the guile to challenge the best in the First Division and Europe, and they did so repeatedly and with success. I think good-quality foreign players can have an enormous influence for the good of the game. Look at the benefits Tottenham reaped with their signing of the two Argentine World Cup stars of 1978, Osvaldo Ardiles and Ricardo Villa. We enjoyed a similar boost briefly at West Ham when I signed the Belgium international striker François van der Elst from New York Cosmos. He gave my team a little extra dimension with his superb technique, but the sad thing was that for a lot of the time he was with us Trevor Brooking was suffering with a troublesome pelvic injury. When I signed François I had an idea that he and Trevor would form a very exciting attacking partnership. Unfortunately, it didn't work out that way, but during his time with us he scored a hat trick of quite remarkable goals in a Milk Cup tie against Notts County in 1983. The problem for a lot of foreign players, of course, is that on the Continent they get time on the ball, and some of them find it difficult to adjust to the pace and competitiveness of our game.

Terry Venables, the Tottenham manager, knows more about the Continental game than most of us, having spent three very successful years with Barcelona, one of the world's most famous clubs. I've always admired Terry wherever he's worked. He developed a fine young side at Crystal Palace, took Queen's Park Rangers to the FA Cup Final and the Second Division Championship, and then led Barcelona to the Spanish League title and the European Cup Final.

It's not easy to go abroad, especially to a club like Barcelona, and improvise. But he did it with great success, despite enormous difficulties. But I've always thought of him as a very bright, diligent coach with innovative ideas and an open mind. He's particularly sharp at working out new ideas for set pieces, and he has the knack of putting orthodox players in unorthodox roles. Chris Waddle was a winger or central striker until Terry decided to play him in the area behind the front strikers. For the marker on the opposing side, Waddle became an even more difficult player to contain, and I suspect that a few First Division defenders breathed a sigh of relief when Spurs sold him to Marseille for £4.5 million.

Kenny Dalglish, who had the good fortune to inherit the most successful set-up in English football at Liverpool, has maintained Anfield's stranglehold on the game. He, too, is a shrewd and subtle coach – qualities he had as a player – and likes to give his players roles that pose awkward questions for the opposition. Dalglish recognized that one of the problems for all the coaches in the First Division is that the game is now so well controlled and marshalled in all areas of the field that there is little left for the coach to exploit. Kenny had the foresight to buy Peter Beardsley from Newcastle and John Barnes from Watford, because he knew that, for his team to maintain their dominance, they would require players who could outwit the best-planned defences. Good teams, really good teams, need something a little different, and Beardsley and Barnes gave Liverpool that difference – especially Beardsley! How do you mark him for a start? He's an all-action player. He's in midfield one minute, on the wing the next, up front the next. His type of player causes problems for any team using the zonal marking system.

Although John Barnes is quick and possesses good close control, marking him is a more straightforward proposition for a defender. But he still isn't easy to mark. His skill gives Liverpool a vast number of options. Kenny has created what is essentially a superb passing team, but players like Beardsley and Barnes give them an edge that few other teams can match.

On their day, perhaps Nottingham Forest come close. For me their manager Brian Clough is a unique and charming man. I've sat with him many times after matches and enjoyed his company. If your team won, or played well, he is the first to give you credit. Like me, he appreciates good football and quality players. I like to be excited by teams, and all his teams have done that to me. His Derby County side that won the

First Division Championship in 1972 was superb. He won the Championship again with Nottingham Forest in 1978 and followed that with two European Cup triumphs. He has sustained his success over a long period of time, and when I left West Ham he became the First Division's longest serving manager, having joined Forest in 1975. Despite the image projected by the media, I have always found him most natural and unassuming, a marvellous motivator and highly knowledgeable about the game. I would have to put him among my all-time greats of soccer management. I've known him a long time and, in the football sense at least, we have a lot in common. Like Liverpool, the feature that distinguishes his teams is that they all pass the ball well. The style is simple, but very effective. He also has a knack of unearthing unknown youngsters and turning them into very good players. I think his son Nigel is a good example of what an accomplished manager can achieve with a player. Nigel has become a very promising player, and Brian, just like Terry Venables and Kenny Dalglish, has deployed him in that awkward area short of the other main striker.

George Graham also proved himself a coach who was willing to try new ideas during Arsenal's Championship-winning season of 1988–9. With eight games to go that season, he decided to change his defensive system, abandoning the flat back four and instead playing with a sweeper and two markers, and pushing his full backs, Nigel Winterburn and Lee Dixon, into midfield. At that stage of the season, with so much at stake, it was a bold move. The three centre backs gave his team extra stability and depth in the heart of the defence, so they were immediately less vulnerable. But it's important with that system that you have good full backs, and Graham had them in Winterburn and Dixon. Both adventurous and prepared to push forward, they gave Arsenal a little extra attacking impetus at a vital stage in the Championship race. The wisdom of the tactical change was seen at Anfield in the last game of the season, when Arsenal beat the defending champions Liverpool 2–0 to lift the Championship.

George played in Bertie Mee's double-winning team of 1971, and demands similar qualities of his own team – durability, efficiency and discipline. He also demands team effort, which is essential in the modern game. You need players who do their jobs well within the team framework. As a manager, he also deserves credit for buying well from smaller clubs. Winterburn came from Wimbledon, Dixon and Steve Bould from Stoke, Kevin Richardson from Watford, Brian Marwood from Sheffield Wednesday and Perry Groves from Colchester. For me, that was good management.

Howard Kendall established a sound reputation as a manager with the team he built at Everton and, of course, he had the good fortune to play in that marvellous midfield, alongside Alan Ball and Colin Harvey, in the superb Harry Catterick team that took the Championship to Goodison Park in 1970.

From the same era, I enjoyed watching Sir Matt Busby's Manchester United team, Bill Nicholson's Tottenham, Bill Shankly's Liverpool and the Manchester City team put together by Joe Mercer and Malcolm Allison.

All these men, of course, left a legacy at their clubs and helped mould today's teams. Nicholson laid the foundations for the modern-day Tottenham, Shankly for the modern Liverpool. There is a similarity, too, between the styles of

Busby's United and today's United, managed so astutely by Alex Ferguson, who I consider a very capable man in every aspect of the game. Alex enjoyed great success at Aberdeen, building a sound team around players of the quality of Jim Leighton, Alex McLeish, Willie Miller, Gordon Strachan and Steve Archibald. He created his own success, establishing an extensive scouting network at schoolboy level in Scotland. His rewards included the European Cup Winners' Cup and the Premier Division championship, and eventually a move to one of the most glamorous clubs in the world, Manchester United. At Old Trafford he has benefited enormously from the financial resources of one of the game's richest clubs. Few managers could spend, as he did, around £6 million in the space of four months, on Neil Webb, Michael Phelan, Gary Pallister and Paul Ince.

Another Scot whom I hold in the highest esteem is Jim McLean, the chairman-manager of Dundee United. He is one of the most industrious and diligent people in the game, but it wasn't until I signed Ray Stewart from his club that I realized just how many hours he devotes to football. Since we became friends he has taken on board the duties of club chairman as well as manager, but I have no doubt that had he decided to join one of the big English clubs he would have been another highly successful Scottish import.

Like Shankly, Nicholson and Busby, Ron Greenwood laid the foundations for the present-day West Ham. Ted Fenton took the club into the First Division and established a youth policy – no mean achievement in those days – but Ron then gave the club a special place in history and a world-wide reputation for entertaining football. He had a long and reward-ing career as manager at Upton Park. He took over in April

1961 – he was previously chief coach at Arsenal – and was in sole charge until 1974, when he pulled me to one side one day and told me that he felt it was time I took charge of first-team affairs. He wanted to continue at the club as general manager, but the responsibility for training and selecting the team would now be mine. In my heart of hearts I had hoped that he would want me to take over one day, but I was surprised when he told me. Of course I wanted to be manager, but I was in no hurry. I was enjoying my life at that time. But the challenge was put in front of me and I willingly accepted it. My contract at the time as assistant manager was worth £80 a week, and we discussed whether I should have a new contract. I was happy with my terms at that time and told the club so. I remained on those terms.

Ron remained as general manager, commuting up from Brighton to deal with matters of finance and scouting. Our relationship really didn't change. He would still give me advice, I would still ask for it; we would discuss what type of players we needed to buy. He was still very much involved and an influential part of the club. Maybe, after all those years of pulling on a tracksuit and sitting in the dug-out, day after day, week after week, he was looking for a new role, a new challenge. If that's what he wanted, he certainly got it. In the summer of 1977, after the shock departure of the England manager Don Revie to the Middle East, Ron and I were in Majorca with West Ham for a pre-season tournament. He had been general manager for three years. We had been on the island only a couple of days when he called me to his hotel room and said: 'I might be leaving. The Football Association has asked me to take temporary charge of the England team.' I was almost as pleased as he was. He had done so much good in the game and it was nice to see him at last get the recognition he deserved. I think he was becoming a bit disillusioned with the game, but suddenly the England job presented him with the challenge he was seeking.

When he told me he was leaving, I knew I would miss him. I remembered the way he had put his arm around Yvonne on Euston Station on the way home from West Ham's FA Cup semifinal win over Manchester United in 1964. My playing career had just finished, and he had every right to be beside himself with joy that evening. But, in the milling crowd on the platform, he found Yvonne and me and said: 'You're the people I'm concerned about. Try not to worry about the future.'

I remembered, too, the way he used to entertain the media poeple in his office after a match at Upton Park. They were informal gatherings, but I enjoyed them immensely and they gave me an invaluable opportunity to sit in the background, look and listen, and appreciate the relationship between a football manager and the media. I served the drinks on those occasions and said little, but learned a lot. I would miss his friendship, his companionship, his advice and his wisdom.

In five successful years as England manager, Ron qualified for the finals of the European Championship and the 1982 World Cup in Spain. He retired, aged 60, after that World Cup. Before the England squad departed for Spain, Eddie Baily, who was scouting for Ron at the time, told me that I was invited to join the FA coaching staff at their training headquarters at the West Lodge Park Hotel near Cockfosters. Ron was giving a small dinner party for people like Don Howe, Eddie and the England physiotherapists Fred Street and Norman Medhurst. I told Eddie that I was honoured to be invited by Ron but, as I was not part of the FA set-up, I felt I had to decline. Back came the message from Eddie: 'Ron says if you're not there you'll be in trouble.' So I went along and had a wonderful, nostalgic evening with him and his staff.

Today Ron lives in quiet retirement in Brighton with his wife, Lucy, and we are still close friends. They spend their time travelling, watching football, or with the families of their children Neil and Carol. On the day West Ham sacked me, he spoke to me on the telephone for ninety minutes. He put it all in perspective. He is a unique man, and I would never have been a football manager but for him.

On the day he left West Ham to join England in 1977 I suddenly felt lonely. For the first time I was on my own. In that first week there simply weren't enough hours in the day for me. I felt I had everything to do. It was now all my responsibility . . . transfers, contracts, scouting, assessing, training, team selection . . .

I remember once asking him: 'What's it really like to be manager, Ron?'

He replied: 'You'll never know until you're on your own.'

THE MOORE, HURST AND PETERS LEGACY

It was difficult at first. My opening match as team manager was against Billy Bingham's Everton in August 1974. We lost 3–2 at Upton Park, and I remember standing in the foyer afterwards explaining the defeat to the media. They wanted to know whether I was going to change the players or the tactics. At that moment I wasn't sure myself, because news of my accession had broken prematurely in the *Evening Standard*. It was due to have been announced officially at a press conference a few days after the Everton game. But immediately it became public knowledge, Ron Greenwood handed control of team matters to me. In the match programme for the following home game – another defeat, 2–1 against Sheffield United – the club stated: 'At a recent board meeting the directors appointed John Lyall as team manager. This was on the recommendation of Ron Greenwood.'

Yes, I was a little apprehensive at this time, but I knew I had the benefit of a superb apprenticeship and, of course, I still had Ron's year's of experience to call upon. Within a month, the results were improving significantly. I lost Trevor Brooking with a broken nose, but in the first week of September, Ron signed a striker, Billy Jennings, from Watford, for £110,000, and a winger, Keith Robson, from Newcastle, for £45,000. They went straight into the team.

We beat Leicester City 6–2 at Upton Park, Jennings scoring twice and Robson once. Four days later we beat Birmingham City 3–0, Jennings and Robson again scoring. The following Saturday we travelled to Burnley, and Robson scored twice and Jennings once in a 5–3 win. In between those First Division games, we beat Tranmere Rovers 6–0 in the second-round replay of the League Cup at Upton Park, Bobby Gould supplying a hat-trick. On 8 October I received a letter on the distinguished notepaper of Arthur Bell and Sons, Ltd, informing me rather grandly that I had been nominated as Manager of the Month for September 1974. I felt I was beginning to find my feet.

Mind you, having worked regularly for years with players of the quality of Geoff Hurst, Martin Peters, Bobby Moore and Johnny Byrne, I knew that I could not have been better prepared for the role. The question now, of course, was could we continue that tradition of nurturing talent of quite exceptional standard. I knew that would be a formidable task.

As a trio with one club, Hurst, Moore and Peters were unique. They were players of skill and intellect. They were quite superb and, like all confident players, had great belief in themselves. But they acknowledged their fame and glory in a self-effacing manner, though there were times, when the team was playing particularly well, when they became a little boisterous. On one such occasion we were preparing for a difficult game against Leeds at Elland Road, and I felt I needed to bring them down to earth a little. Ron had left me in charge of training that day, and I devised a routine that was difficult but probably just within their capabilities. If they failed to do it I would have made a little point – none of us are perfect, lads – but if they succeeded I would have to hold up my hands in admiration. I used the entire length of a training pitch at Chadwell Heath, with a goalkeeper at one end and Hurst, Moore and Peters strung across the width of the pitch at the other. They had to pass the ball between them as they worked the ball the length of the field – and then score. The catch was that the ball wasn't allowed to touch the ground at any stage and each player, on receiving, had only one touch. In other words, they had to volley or head their passes between them from one goal to the other using the width of the pitch. Most of the other team members were on the sidelines speculating about the degree of difficulty and who was most likely to fail among these three great players. None failed. They did it, first time, and I held my hands up in admiration.

I arrived as a youngster at West Ham a year before Bobby and, although it was plain to see he had enormous potential, you simply couldn't envisage the sort of career that was to follow for him. We were great pals. As teenagers together, we young lads used to go dancing in our shiny mohair suits at the Ilford Palais, and Bobby, as immaculate as ever, always looked just a little cut above everyone else.

If we were out late I often stayed with Bobby at his parents' house in Barking. No matter what time we arrived home he always carefully brushed down his suit before he went to bed. He was just as fastidious as a player. Albert Walker, Ron's team attendant, used to give each first-team player a pair of tie-ups for his socks before the first match of the season. Most players, when they returned to the dressing room after the match, would throw them into a muddy pile and expect another pair before the next home game. Not Bobby! He picked the mud off the tie-ups, folded them

above Mum and dad in the lounge of their home in Wanstead.

below Where it all began – me with the ball *(front row, third from left)* with the Parkhill Primary School team. Tom Carter, the schoolteacher on the left, was the man who lectured me on the power of positive thinking – both in sport and in education.

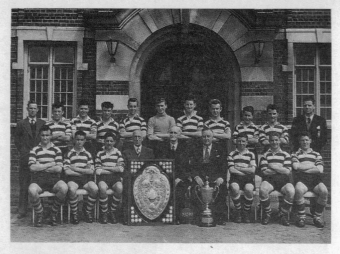

above Ilford Schools team, with me sitting far right. Stan Frankland *(standing, far left)* was the coach and motivator, who used to cycle alongside the boys during training runs.

below A rare goal, playing for Ilford Schools at Cricklefields Stadium, Ilford. Just behind me you can see Mickey Harrison, who became a professional with Chelsea, Blackburn, Plymouth and Luton.

West Ham United Football Co., Limited

MANAGER
E. B. A. FENTON

SECRETARY
F. H. CEARNS

REGISTERED OFFICE
BOLEYN GROUND
GREEN STREET
UPTON PARK, E.13

Your Ref.

Our Ref. EBAF/PM

30th July, 1955.

J. Lyall Snr.,
12a, Claybury Parade,
Woodford Green, E.

Dear Mr. Lyall,

     This is to confirm that your Son John will commence work here in the Office on Tuesday 2nd August at 9.0 a.m. at a commencing wage of £4. 0. 0. per week.

     It is also a condition of the employment that he is allowed time off to go to school to study in preparation for taking his General Schools Certificate. I am sure you will appreciate my suggestion to the latter which will be to his benefit in the future.

               Yours sincerely,

               E.B.A. FENTON,
               Manager.

My first letter of employment, sent to my father by Ted Fenton, then manager of West Ham.

above The happiest day of my life – Yvonne and I outside St George's Church, Gants Hill, on our wedding day in 1961. John Bond is stealing a kiss from the bride, watched, from the terraces so to speak, by *(left to right)* Albert Walker, Malcolm Musgrove, Ron Greenwood, Andy Malcolm, Ken Brown, Brian Rhodes, John Dick, Bill Jenkins, Joe Kirkup and Ernie Gregory. Few people will realize that this picture spans half a century of West Ham's history. Albert Walker was a stout-hearted defender from Lancashire when he joined the club in 1932, and was first-team attendant when he retired at Upton Park in 1980. Ernie Gregory joined the ground-staff in 1936 and after a distinguished goalkeeping career with West Ham retired from the coaching staff in 1987.

opposite, top How many famous faces can you spot in this photograph of Ron Greenwood's first squad at West Ham? *Back (left to right)*: Joe Kirkup, me, John Bond, Lawrie Leslie, Ken Brown, Bill Lansdowne, Bobby Moore. *Centre (left to right)*: Tony Scott, Phil Woosnam, Alan Sealey, Malcolm Musgrove, Ian Crawford, John Dick. *Front (left to right)*: Eddie Bovington, Jack Burkett, Martin Peters, Ronnie Boyce.
opposite, bottom The old Chicken Run at Upton Park provides a nostalgic background as Geoff Hurst and I challenge for a high ball in a reserve game against Tottenham.

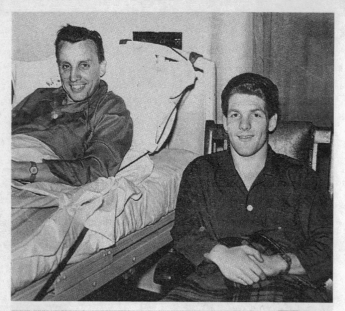

opposite, top It's nice to have a friend with you in hospital. This is me recovering from my first knee operation in the London Hospital in 1959. Vic Keeble was also recovering from a knee operation.

above It was a lonely road back to fitness, and I spent weeks running up and down the terracing on the North Bank at Upton Park after my first knee operation. It's a gruelling routine used to build up stamina and wasted muscles, and years later, as a manager, I always felt a few pangs of sympathy for a player going through this rehabilitation exercise. It's boring, lonely and very hard work.

opposite, bottom It's not all fun. This was West Ham against Tottenham on Boxing Day, 1963. We lost 3–0 and I was knocked out. I was learning the hard way.

above Teacher and pupil – Ron Greenwood and me at West Ham's Chadwell Heath training headquarters in my early days as assistant manager.

below Ron Greenwood and Mr Pratt, the club chairman, were two of the most influential figures in the early years of my career at West Ham.

neatly and tucked them into his boots. At the end of each season he had the same pair of tie-ups he started with. He was just as careful about tucking a clean white handkerchief into his shorts before each match. Those little things illustrate how diligently he looked after the details in his life. He devoted the same detail to his game. As a player he had immense foresight, vision and knowledge. He had an enquiring mind, and what he learned, particularly from Ron, helped make him one of the great international captains. He liked to play the game properly, and he led both England and West Ham by example. He could see and interpret correctly everything that was happening on the pitch. That's what gave him such wonderful vision. He was always looking for the space to play the ball into. If he couldn't see it in front of him or on the wings, he was happy to play the ball back to his own goalkeeper, knowing this would draw the opposition out of their defensive positions and create space for West Ham's attackers.

He was also a great interceptor, one of the best I've ever seen in the game. He didn't have to tackle very often, because he invariably knew where the ball was going – and he would be there first. I've seen a lot of very fast players who went nowhere, like headless chickens. Bobby wasn't very fast, but he had a quicker brain than anyone else on the pitch. He knew he wasn't very fast, but he worked prodigiously hard at his sprinting during our training sessions. I never knew him shirk a challenge. If you told him he was vulnerable in the air, he would go out on a Saturday afternoon, outjump everyone and win all the high balls. With such a man, it was no surprise that he went on to captain England in their World Cup Final victory over West Germany and win 108 international caps. As he became one of the world's greatest players, our careers inevitably followed different paths, but he has remained a good and valued friend to this day.

As a young coach, I appreciated the way he helped make my task easier. I remember being put in charge of the team for a foreign trip for the first time in May 1971. I was assistant manager, and the club had agreed to go on an eleven-match four-week tour of the United States. Ron knew he would be busy in London that summer, so he asked me to take charge. He felt it would be a good experience for me. It was no easy task for the players at the end of a long season – particularly for Bobby, who had spent the previous summer at the World Cup Finals in Mexico and most of the summers before that on duty with England. I took all the senior players, including Geoff Hurst, another uncomplaining England workhorse who would have probably preferred a restful summer, Ronnie Boyce, Bryan Robson, Frank Lampard, Clyde Best, Billy Bonds and Bobby Ferguson.

Soon after we arrived in the States, Bobby came to me and said: 'John, do whatever you want. I'll play every game if you want. Don't feel you have to substitute me, either, unless you want to do it for tactical reasons.' He played all eleven games for me. I sensed that he wanted to help me make a success of my career. The other lads felt the same way. It was all part of the family atmosphere at Upton Park.

Despite world-wide fame Bobby was an unassuming man. Those who don't know him have suggested that he's aloof, but nothing could be further from the truth. As a player at West Ham he wanted to be treated like all the others and would often put his teammates before himself. I remember on that trip to the United States in 1971, standing in the bar of a Los Angeles hotel with Bobby and the entire first-team squad. I'd given the players a couple of days off between matches, and they were enjoying a quiet, relaxing evening. At the end of the evening the waiter produced the bill for the drinks, and Bobby took it quietly and said: 'I'll pay.' I told him it wasn't necessary because all the lads were receiving a daily spending allowance, but he insisted.

When he finally retired from playing, I was surprised that he didn't pursue a managerial career more vigorously, because he had the experience, temperament, knowledge and love of the game that is required in management, and he was also a qualified FA coach. But perhaps players of Bobby's status in the game can diversify when they retire and don't need to devote their time to management.

Geoff Hurst was from a similar mould. The way he responded in training gave me enormous confidence. He came to West Ham as a wing half from Chelmsford, and at that stage, you could never imagine him re-writing the history books with a hat trick in the World Cup Final. He was a powerful, confident lad, a good all-round sportsman who played County cricket for Essex. When he was a wing half in West Ham's reserves, we played a number of games together. He never looked entirely comfortable in that role. I think he would be the first to admit that he thought of himself as more of an attacking player than a defensive one. But he had excellent technique for such a big man, and raw strength gave a competitive edge to his game. Ron obviously realized we were not getting the best out of him and decided to try him as a central striker alongside Johnny Byrne. Ron knew he would have to work hard with him on the training ground and he did just that, eventually using Geoff as the focal point of his near-post-cross tactic. Determination and aggression were the qualities that underpinned Geoff's game. He wanted to succeed, and he worked as hard as Bobby on the training ground. He developed into an outstanding, very coachable striker, who Ron, in later years as England manager, used to demonstrate skills and tactics to his international stars.

There are few players of 6 ft who can be both physically commanding and possess superb technique. Geoff had both qualities. His years as a wing half had taught him the value of mobility, and this made him an unselfish team player. He would run wide to create space for others or, with his back to goal, would draw teammates into the play. And, when facing goal, his pace, power and courage took him into the most difficult situations. He was the outstanding, all-round striker of his era and would be priceless in the modern age when strikers are basically pigeon-holed in two categories. They are either the target man or the goalscorer who feeds off him. Geoff could fill both roles. I still see him from time to time, usually when he visits the Chadwell Heath training ground to get footballs autographed by the present team. He's now a very successful businessman and I generally have a gentle dig at him when he asks his old teammate, Ronnie Boyce, to get the balls signed.

'Have you paid Ronnie for the balls, Geoff?' I asked him one day.

'I'll pay him tomorrow when I pick them up,' he replied.

'Geoff,' I said. 'Ronnie can't afford to splash out on footballs just like that, you know. He's not an executive like you. I think you'd better leave your watch with him.'

Without a murmur, Geoff took off his watch and presented

it to Ronnie as security. Next day he came back, picked up his footballs and his watch, and paid Ronnie.

For many years Geoff worked in the same motor-insurance business as Martin Peters. They were always close, as players and friends. Martin was as talented as any player I've ever seen, and his determination to succeed was fuelled by a deep love of the game. As a young lad he would be the first player to arrive at the training ground and would then implore any other early starters to work with him out on the pitch before the organized training began. I remember, one Friday morning at Upton Park, watching him and Harry Redknapp playing about together. Harry was crossing from the corner flag and Martin was almost lazily volleying the ball into the back of the net. It was something that came naturally to him. As I watched them I heard Martin shout to Harry.

'Chip one in, and I'll hit the crossbar.' Harry centred the ball and Martin drove his shot, first time, smack against the crossbar.

'Lucky!' Harry shouted. Martin just smiled.

'I bet you 5 to 1 you can't do it again,' cried Harry, who enjoyed a little wager occasionally.

Martin accepted, and when the ball came over – a perfect centre to be fair to Harry – Martin drove it, first time, smack against the crossbar. By this time Harry was a little perplexed, not to mention concerned about his money.

'Double or nothing,' he shouted.

Again Martin accepted. Again the ball came across, falling nicely in front of him, about waist high, and Martin volleyed it straight against the crossbar – three times out of three.

He was a special player with a special talent. The fact that he wore every shirt for West Ham, from the goalkeeper's jersey to number 11, illustrated his immense versatility. He was a European type of player, comfortable and secure in any position. Subtle, sleek, athletic, elusive, he used to sneak in almost unseen at the back post to score spectacular goals. He still looks only 28 today, and if you see him in charity matches he still displays all the flair and touch he had in his great years.

It was sad to see him leave West Ham, but I think he felt that it was time to establish his own identity in the game. For years it had been Moore, Hurst and Peters, in that order, and Martin felt it was time to show he could succeed at another club. Valued at £200,000, he joined Spurs in a part-exchange deal that brought the legendary Jimmy Greaves to Upton Park. I'd known Jim for years, followed his progress from his schoolboy days, and admired his unrivalled goalscoring ability. But when I first played against him in the Corinthian Shield Under-15s Final, he wasn't a goalscorer at all. He was playing for Dagenham Schools, and he ran my Ilford team ragged. He had a dribbling talent and a passing talent that was way and above anything else on the field that day. Back in the fifties, all the youngsters wanted to dribble like Stanley Matthews. It didn't matter if you failed to score a goal, but if you made ten you were a hero. Jimmy dribbled rings round us that day and, although he didn't score, someone obviously spotted a talent that could be exploited. Soon after that game he was playing in the Chelsea youth team. They had obviously realized that if they could add a goalscoring ability to his approach work they would have an outstanding player. And that's what he became. Throughout his career he created many of his own goals, weaving through thickets of defenders to gently slide the ball past the goalkeeper. Of course, he also scored with tap-ins from close range and first-time strikes from the edge of the area, but many of his most spectacular goals were those he created himself with his tight ball control.

Jim was a delightful, infectious character, a very nice man, who scored twice for West Ham on his debut in a 5–2 win over Manchester City at Maine Road. That was the game in which Ronnie Boyce got hold of a clearance from the City goalkeeper, Joe Corrigan, in the centre circle and volleyed it straight back into the net. Joe had turned round and was walking back to the goal. He thought the ball he saw nestling in the back of the net had been left there from half time. Jimmy was so delighted with his two goals that day that I remember him asking Ron if he could wear his number 10 shirt on the journey home.

Sadly, we didn't see the best of him at West Ham. He had suffered with hepatitis, a debilitating illness, late in his career at Tottenham, and that had diluted his sharpness in the penalty area. Jimmy always says that if you ask Chelsea supporters which were his best years they will say those at Chelsea. If you ask Spurs supporters, they will say those at Spurs. But if you ask West Ham supporters they will say those at either Chelsea or Spurs. His brief career at West Ham spanned just two seasons – he scored thirteen goals in thirty-six matches – and he decided to retire from the game in 1971, at the age of 31. It's a testament to his strength of character that he went on to overcome difficult personal problems, and became a household name as a television personality.

Johnny Byrne was of a similar nature – bright, confident, full of humour and mischief. Ron Greenwood paid a then

British record fee of £65,000 to sign him from Crystal Palace, and to begin with he had a difficult time. His problem was that he was trying to take the lace out of the ball every time he got into the penalty area. He had to be taught to do the simple things. In his early days I remember watching him wriggle past defenders, walk around the goalkeeper and then miss an empty net. Ron told him to go back to basics, and it probably took a year of hard work on the training ground before we began to get the best out of him. There's no doubt that once Ron got the message across, 'Budgie' became an outstanding striker. He was known as 'Budgie' throughout his career at West Ham because he never stopped talking. He chirped, just like a budgerigar. He was at his chirpiest one November night in 1966, when he masterminded the 7–0 demolition of Leeds United in the League Cup at Upton Park. That was the Leeds United of Bremner, Hunter, Charlton and Giles. It was an irresistible performance by West Ham, and Byrne in particular.

There's no doubt that he became an outstanding player. He took up such marvellous positions that Bobby Moore could find him in the dark. He also had a great influence on the development of Geoff Hurst as a central striker. They formed a magnificent goalscoring partnership. I think Geoff first realized the full value of controlling the ball with the chest, a hallmark of his game, when he watched Budgie doing it. He would take the ball on his chest and, before it reached the ground, volley it out to the wings. He also had a wonderful sense of timing that enabled him to outjump taller defenders.

There is a tendency to look back over the years and get the merits and achievements of great players of another era out of perspective. Time perhaps gives a gloss to some careers that is not always fully deserved. But I believe that even in today's well-organized, athletic and disciplined game, those players would have thrived. More than that, they would have achieved the superstar status they enjoyed in their own playing days. I think Jimmy Greaves today would be one of the hardest strikers to mark, and would still score goals at a prolific rate. Bobby Moore would still be the supreme defender. Moore, Hurst, Peters, Byrne and Greaves could all improvise, and I am convinced that, assuming they had today's levels of fitness, they could adapt their styles and have successful careers. They all had that essential ingredient, skill with the ball, and because of their level of ability all would adapt to the demands of the game in whatever era they played.

It was perhaps appropriate that one of the chief examiners in my own first season as manager of West Ham was my old pal Bobby Moore. He had played the last of his 700-odd games for West Ham in an FA Cup third-round tie against Hereford in January 1974, and joined Fulham two months later. The following season, 1974–5, while I was coming to terms with my new role as team manager, he and former England colleague Alan Mullery were the cornerstones of the Fulham side that reached the FA Cup Final. Their charge to Wembley included two notable First Division scalps – first Everton, and then Birmingham City in the semifinal.

West Ham's season in the First Division, after that encouraging September when I was voted Manager of the Month, had been indifferent, though the new signings, Jennings and Robson, had shared twenty-three goals. Funnily enough, in October that season, Second Division Fulham, with Moore and Mullery outstanding, had beaten West Ham 2–1 in the third round of the League Cup at Craven Cottage. There were lessons from that match that were to stand me in good stead later in the season.

The bonus, of course, that season was our own form in the FA Cup. I was already aware that the team needed strengthening, and the benefit of the partnership I then had with Ron was that, while I was with the first team on a Saturday afternoon, he could travel round the country casting his eyes over good young players. One day Ron told me about a youngster called Alan Taylor who was playing for Rochdale in the Fourth Division. He was raw, he said, but very quick, and he felt we could develop his talent. In November that season West Ham paid £40,000 for him and, just as Ron said, he proved to be devastatingly fast. He was a former motor mechanic from Morecambe, who had learned the basics of his football in the Northern Premier League before signing for Rochdale. We obviously needed to work with him on the training ground, but he had a good attitude, and the fact that many years later he was still playing for Norwich at the age of 34 speaks volumes for his enthusiasm. With typical East End humour, the other lads at the club nicknamed him 'Sparrow' because of his thin legs. He didn't get into the team immediately. We won 2–1 at Southampton in the third round of the FA Cup in January, and a few weeks later, after a 1–1 draw at Upton Park, beat Swindon 2–1 in the replay. In round five we beat Queen's Park Rangers 2–1 at Upton Park, and then, inevitably, we were in among the big boys. The quarter-final pitted us against Arsenal at Highbury. We had lost there 3–0 in a First Division match back in October. I went to watch them before the cup-tie and felt that we could expose the left side of their defence if we attacked them with pace. I decided then to play Alan Taylor. At that time he had made just three appearances for us, two of them as substitute, and although I had started with him in a match at Stoke the previous December I had taken him off. It was something of a gamble, especially as the player he would replace was the experienced Bobby Gould, who worked so hard and did a terrific job for us. I admired Bobby's attitude as a player, and it's easy to understand now why he has been so successful in management.

I felt, though, that Alan's pace might prove to be a key element of the game. He was also a completely unknown quantity to most rival managers in Division One, whereas Bobby Gould had spent two years in Arsenal's first team. The rest, of course, has been well catalogued. Alan scored both goals in our 2–0 win at Highbury. I had to keep him in the side, obviously, and he repaid me handsomely. In the semifinal we drew 0–0 with Bobby Robson's very good Ipswich side at Villa Park. We went to Stamford Bridge for the replay and, amid swirling snow, Alan scored two more to give us a 2–1 victory and secure a place in the FA Cup Final.

I relished the prospect of an all-London Final against Fulham, especially as Bobby Moore would be masterminding their fortunes on the field. Off the field, of course, they had the benefit of the vastly experienced manager Alec Stock to call upon. As far as I was concerned, our pre-match plan was quite straightforward – we simply had to keep the ball away from Bobby Moore. We felt if we allowed him too much of the ball he would control the game. I still had a great deal of respect for him, even though he was 34, and I knew that if he and Mullery had half a chance they would cause us problems. I stressed to my players how important it was to pressure these two experienced former England men if they got hold of the ball. Keith Robson was injured and I decided to play Pat Holland wide on the left, because I knew he could curl the ball into the middle but keep it away from Bobby in the heart of the Fulham defence.

When the big day came it passed too quickly. I was manager in my first season in charge, and here I was, leading the team out for the FA Cup Final at Wembley. There had been no debate with Ron on that point. He told me that he expected me to lead the team out of the tunnel and on to the pitch. It is truly a remarkable experience, but at the time you don't really appreciate it. Afterwards, though, you feel the elation. It's a champagne day, not just for you and your players, but for everyone from the club – the cleaners, the laundry ladies, the administration staff, the fans.

West Ham were in the rather unusual position of being considered favourites, and that meant I had to get the preparation exactly right. I think it was right. Sadly, the game was no classic. We won 2–0, and had it not been for the experience of Moore and Mullery, Fulham might have suffered a heavier defeat. It was a wonderful way for two great professionals to end their careers.

But the day really belonged to Alan Taylor. Six months earlier he had been unknown. But his two goals for West Ham at Wembley that day elevated him to national-hero status. It was real Roy of the Rovers stuff. At the club banquet in the West End that evening I remember thinking to myself: 'Well, if every season's like this, I won't complain.'

Of course, I was soon to learn that days like that are few in the life of a football manager. The West Ham playing staff had changed enormously in the previous four or five years.

The days of Hurst, Moore and Peters were over. But we had a big crop of locally produced players like Trevor Brooking, Pat Holland, John McDowell, Frank Lampard and Kevin Lock, plus a handful signed from other clubs – Billy Bonds from Charlton Athletic, Bobby Ferguson from Kilmarnock, Tommy Taylor from Leyton Orient, Graham Paddon from Norwich, and Taylor, Jennings and Robson. Not all of them were blessed with the unique talents of a Moore or Greaves, but they all made the very best of what they had to offer. Every team needs a blend and a balance, and those players gave as much to the club as the most distinguished internationals. It said much for the family atmosphere at West Ham that the great trio of Hurst, Moore and Peters would stress at every opportunity the debt they owed to emerging youngsters like Brooking, Lampard and Holland.

My second season as team manager, 1975–6, much like my first to be honest, was less than successful in the First Division. We started brightly enough – top of the table in November after just two defeats in our opening fifteen matches – but once we became enmeshed in the European Cup-Winners' Cup we slumped disastrously. We didn't win any of our last sixteen First Division matches and we finished eighteenth in the table. Dominating everything that season were our adventures in Europe. It was my first taste of European football as a manager, but I had the benefit of being able to call upon the expertise of Ron and his assistant, Bill Nicholson, both wise in the ways of Continental football and its pitfalls. I learned the lessons of European football quickly. I had to.

We faced Reipas Lahti of Finland in the first round, and everyone told me we would get through easily. We travelled to Finland for the first leg and just scraped a 2–2 draw. It was a big disappointment. I remember calling the players up to my hotel room after the match. They were very subdued, and I felt I needed to put it into perspective for them.

'It hasn't gone the way we hoped,' I said. 'But we get another bite at them. Let's make sure we learn the lessons and do the job properly next time.' A lot of them were youngsters and I think they felt they had let me down. We got it right in the return leg, beating the Finns 3–0 at Upton Park, with goals from Keith Robson, Pat Holland and Billy Jennings.

The second round presented a far more daunting prospect – a trip to the Soviet Union to play Ararat Erevan, a city in the republic of Armenia in the Caucasus Mountains. It is one of the oldest cities in the world and not far from Mount Ararat, where Noah's Ark is supposed to have come to rest after the Great Flood. Well, at the end of the first leg, I was in desperate need of a bit of divine guidance. Alan Taylor scored for us after fifty-six minutes, but the Soviets equalized with one of the most amazing goals I've ever seen. Mervyn Day, holding the ball firmly in his hands, was being harrassed by Nazar Petrosian. As Mervyn prepared to throw the ball out, Petrosian lunged forward and headed it from between his hands. In a flurry of arms and legs, the Erevan striker then drove the ball over the goal-line. I naturally assumed that we would be awarded a free kick for a foul on our goalkeeper. Instead, the referee, Hans Weyland of West Germany, awarded Erevan a goal, much to the amusement of a 66,000 crowd. I couldn't believe it. If Noah had been around at that moment I'd have drowned him.

That evening we were invited to a dinner given by the host club. Our interpreter, George Scanlon of Liverpool University, a languages expert used by many football clubs, proceeded during the speeches to lecture the sheepish Soviet dignitories on bad sportsmanship. We returned to England with a 1–1 draw, and with a sense of moral indignation, duly despatched the Soviets 3–1 in the second leg at Upton Park. I felt justice had been done.

In the quarter-finals we were drawn to meet Den Haag of Holland. The first leg was away, and during the course of the afternoon on the day of the match I began to feel unwell, and went to bed in the hotel. We had trained in the morning and I had given the team talk, but at about five in the evening our physiotherapist, Rob Jenkins, checked me over, declared I had a virus and a temperature of 103° and told me that it would be unwise to go to the match. I stayed in bed and Ron took over.

At half-time we were 4–0 down. In those situations the players often look to the coach for guidance in the dressing room. The man they were looking at on this occasion was Ron Greenwood. He had been through it so many times. He knew exactly what to do. He knew we had to attack in the second half to have any chance in the return leg. He took Mick McGiven off, replaced him with Keith Coleman, changed the team tactically, and we flew home the next day knowing that we still had a chance. Ron's tactical changes helped Billy Jennings score two goals. We lost 4–2, but it could have been far worse. I knew the Dutch would find the atmosphere in our cramped little ground at Upton Park difficult to cope with in the second leg. We had a crowd of 30,000 squeezed into the stadium, and I think the Dutch found the occasion intimidating. We won 3–1 to leave the score as 5–5 on aggregate. We went through to the semifinals on the away-goals rule.

Eintracht Frankfurt, an accomplished West German team with players like Holzenbein, Grabowski and Nickel, provided formidable opposition in the semifinal. We lost the first leg in Frankfurt 2–1 – Graham Paddon scored the West Ham goal – but the return leg at Upton Park was a night to remember. We played on a wet top, the ball moved quickly, and Brooking was superb. He scored twice and Keith Robson got the other as we won 3–1 in front of a wall-to-wall crowd of nearly 40,000.

In the final in the Heysel Stadium, the scene years later of the terrible European Cup Final tragedy, we faced Anderlecht of Belgium. A player who was later to join West Ham probably destroyed us that evening. I refer, of course, to François van der Elst, who looked a quite outstanding player when Ron and I went to watch Anderlecht before the final. Nearly 60,000 fans filled the Heysel Stadium – 10,000 had travelled from London – and they saw Pat Holland give West Ham the lead after twenty-eight minutes. But, just before half-time, Frank Lampard misjudged a backpass to Mervyn Day, allowing Ressel to intercept. He switched the ball to Rensenbrink who hammered in the equalizer.

But the real tragedy of the incident was that in playing the ball back Frank had torn a stomach muscle and had to miss the rest of the game. That, plus the fact we were facing an uphill battle against outstanding opponents like Rensenbrink, Haan, Van Binst, Vercauteren and van der Elst, proved just too big a hurdle. Van der Elst put the Belgians in front just before half time and, although Robson equalized, van der Elst and Rensenbrink both scored again after the interval. We lost 4–2, but it was a wonderful game of football and I felt we had upheld the nation's reputation in our first European final since 1965.

I was learning to be grateful for the good times. Our form in the First Division was again indifferent and it was worrying me. We started 1976–7 badly, with only one win from our first twelve games. Perhaps what made the biggest impression on me, though, was the 6–0 thrashing we suffered at Sunderland. It was March and they were in trouble with us at the bottom of the table. We both had nineteen points, but they had played two games more. They seemed, though, to be getting out of trouble, having scored eleven goals in three successive wins against Bristol City, Middlesbrough and West Bromwich Albion before facing West Ham. Not long before, we had signed Bryan Robson for the second time – on this occasion from Sunderland – but unfortunately he missed the visit to Roker Park because of injury. I don't think it would have made any significant difference had he played. We were appalling. It was one of the worst performances in my career as a manager. I was furious with the players afterwards, and it was an anger that seemed to burn more fiercely as we drove home on the coach. It was our worst defeat since Burnley had beaten us by the same score at Turf Moor in 1962. On the journey home I sat alongside Mr Pratt at the front of the coach. As we sped past a motorway service station I said to him: 'We are going to pull into the next service station we come to, and I'm going to get all the players off the coach and they can find their own way home.'

Mr Pratt, a chairman who hated losing, looked across at me.

'Do you think no manager has ever lost 6–0 before,' he said, without the slightest trace of emotion. 'If you want to be a good manager you must learn to accept defeat. The secret is to rectify the mistakes the following week.'

He told me to sit back, relax, and think about what he had just said. He was right, of course. When I got back to Upton Park that night I had got it all in a proper perspective. But for a while that night I was prepared to leave the team stranded at a service station in the far north. Looking back on it, I could have made a rash decision that would have seriously affected my relationship with the players. Mr Pratt had been a calming influence. The following week we beat Manchester City 1–0, Bryan Robson scoring the goal. But it was a struggle right until the end of the season. We were unbeaten in our last seven games, but we needed to beat Manchester United at Upton Park in the final match to be sure of staying up. This was the United of Hill, Coppell, Pearson and Greenhoff, heading towards a Wembley victory against Liverpool later in the week. It was an enthralling match that started awfully when we conceded a goal to Gordon Hill after just thirty seconds. But the crowd got behind the team, and we finally won 4–2, with goals from the reliable Robson (two), Frank Lampard and Geoff Pike. At the end the crowd remained on the terraces and demanded that the team re-appear. It was their way of showing their appreciation for a tremendous fightback and the fact that the players had at last salvaged a season that had looked doomed.

Certainly the most encouraging feature of the season had been the discovery of Alan Devonshire. We were tipped off about this skinny lad playing for Southall, and at the start of the season Eddie Baily went to have a look at him. When Eddie told Ron Greenwood that Reading were making overtures to Southall we had to make up our minds. Ron gave Eddie the authority to spend £5,000.

'If there's a lot of activity and you feel we should sign him, do it,' said Ron. 'We'll trust your judgement.'

Eddie and his invaluable assistant, Charlie Faulkner, went back to Southall, and within twenty minutes of their arrival at the ground they had bought him for £5,000. It was one of the best pieces of business the club did during my time there. Mind you, I wasn't so sure about that on the day Alan arrived for his first training session. It was just his misfortune that it was a physical day in the training schedule. I had organized a routine that involved one player doing as many sharp runs as he could up and down the terracing, while his partner did a single lap of the pitch. Alan was a frail-looking lad, and after his first lap around the pitch he collapsed. 'He's not used to it,' we thought. 'He'll get up in a minute.' But he didn't.

I was getting a little concerned when Rob Jenkins came rushing across the pitch to treat him. He revived him and discovered he had a high temperature and a virus. So, having just joined us, he was then off sick for ten days. After training that day, I saw Ron in his office.

'How did the boy Devonshire do?' he asked.

'He collapsed,' I replied.

But once Alan settled into the training routine, he was fine. He played four reserve games, and I remember going to Hereford one night just to watch him in action. I thought that night: 'Blow it. I'm going to play this fellow.' The following week I put him into the side against Queen's Park Rangers in a League Cup tie. We lost 2–0, but he played well.

The following season was disastrous; a nightmare relieved only by the emergence of Devonshire and Geoff Pike, the signing for a club record fee of £180,000 of David Cross from West Bromwich Albion, and the League debut of a young centre half called Alvin Martin late in the season. Towards the latter part of that season I used to spend long hours in discussion with Eddie Baily assessing our own players and drawing comparisons between them and those we might buy. I felt we needed to rebuild; not tinker with the team, but rebuild it substantially.

We started the season badly, with three consecutive defeats and only one win in our first twelve games. We enjoyed a little revival at the very end of the season with six wins from our last nine games. David Cross proved his worth then, with seven goals in his last seven games. I thought for a time we might just get out of trouble: we still had a chance of avoiding relegation in the last game of the season. A 37,000 crowd filled Upton Park. We lost 2–0 and were relegated to Division Two. Our conquerors that day – Liverpool.

THE 1980 CUP FINAL

Relegation was a terrible blow to the club, the players and my own pride. It had been a long and traumatic season. I felt we had a team capable of staying in Division One, and we had so nearly escaped. But if a team's results are inconsistent you have to accept the outcome. In West Ham's case, the outcome meant the end of the club's twenty-year reign in the First Division. At the end of that game against Liverpool, their manager, Bob Paisley, and two of his long-serving staff men, Ronnie Moran and Roy Evans, came into the small office I have next to the dressing rooms at Upton Park. I have always admired the attitude of Liverpool. They are all ordinary men who, despite their phenomenal successes, always play down their victories. They apologized not so much for winning, but for sending us into Division Two. They said they had to try and finish the season above their Merseyside rivals Everton. The win that day gave them fifty-seven points and secured second place behind the champions, Nottingham Forest. Everton were in third place with fifty-five points. We were nowhere. That's the reality of the job.

It was the first major disappointment of my managerial career, and I had to try to keep it in perspective. A few days after the Liverpool match I received a telephone call that helped me considerably. It was from the actress Billie Whitelaw, whose young son was a West Ham fan. From time to time she would bring him to the ground to meet the players. She was, of course, an established star of West End theatre and films, and she told me that she had reached a point where she realized she was no longer examining the qualities of her own performances. She simply took them for granted. At that time she took a decision to look at her career more deeply and make herself work a little harder with people perhaps not quite so efficient or professional. So she went into provincial rep; she moved from the First Division to the Second. She made the decision consciously. We didn't, but she said we might find it had the same effect. She found working in smaller theatres a refreshing and stimulating experience, and it gave her the chance to look at her career and performance in a different light. I have always remembered the advice she gave me in that conversation. I thought to myself: 'Well, maybe some good will come out of relegation.' West Ham were about to perform on a smaller stage, just as she had done. I was determined to make the experience work for me, just as it had done for Billie Whitelaw.

I felt it was important, firstly, not to make rash decisions. I went away with the family for a week's fishing in Norfolk. I have always loved fishing. I started as a youngster and, as a football manager, found it an invaluable form of therapy. My brothers and I used to fish when our parents took us to Scotland for the summer holidays. When I was finally given my own rod, I used to take the bus from Ilford to Abridge and walk up the road to the River Roding. I joined Barkingside Angling Club when I was about 14, and I can remember getting out of bed at 2 a.m. to walk to Ilford station and then catching an early coach for a day's fishing in the country. I'm not really a good angler, because I'm not competitive about it. I go to enjoy myself and relax. I admire the people who sit on a river bank for three or four days hoping for the one bite that will land them a specimen fish, but that's not me. I fish for carp and tench, and I enjoy the riverside atmosphere and the solitude as much as the thrill of catching one. I like the countryside, and just as footballers have idols, I have one of my own – Jack Hargreaves, a real countryman and an accomplished angler, who used to present a television programme called *Out of Town*. These days I don't fish as much as I would like, largely because I've spent a lot of my spare time with my son Murray refurbishing the house Yvonne and I bought in rural Essex. But even there, when we landscaped the garden, we installed fish ponds that we filled with koi carp.

I appreciated the peace and quiet of Norfolk during that week in the summer of 1978. It was then that I decided that we would start our first season in Division Two with, essentially, an unchanged team. I hoped, like all managers in my position must hope, that we would bounce back first time. Looking back, with a little more consistency we would probably have done so. At Christmas we were third in the table, and in February, just before the transfer deadline, I paid that world-record fee for a goalkeeper for Phil Parkes from Queen's Park Rangers. I felt we had a good chance of promotion, and a signing of that magnitude might just fuel the team for what remained of the season. But it was a fiercely contested promotion race that season. When we visited Stoke in March, Parkes's third match for us, just four points covered the top six clubs. It was a significant match, made all the more memorable by an unnerving experience on the coach ride from London the preceding day. Travelling at high speed on the motorway the coach windscreen suddenly shattered and splinters of glass flew half the length of the vehicle. Thankfully, no one was hurt, but our promotion hopes were seriously damaged next day when we lost 2–0 in driving rain. On the strength of that victory, Stoke went to the top of the table.

Although we had games in hand on most of our promotion rivals, we won only one of the next six. Even so, when we visited Blackburn Rovers with three games to go, we still had a chance of snatching a promotion place. We lost 1–0 and, with that result, condemned ourselves to another season in Division Two. We finished fifth. In our situation, just missing out was not good enough.

For the last half a dozen games of that season I asked my assistant Eddie Baily to watch our matches. I wanted a critical assessment of our players. Then, if we failed to win promotion, he could compare those he had seen playing for West Ham with those he had seen playing for other clubs. In this way he could help me decide how we could best strengthen the team. It was clear to me now that we had to make changes. Apart from that, several first-team players were out of contract that summer, and the fact that we were still in Division Two meant that I was unable to offer them substantial salary increases. In a couple of months that summer Alan Curbishley was transferred to Birmingham City, Bryan Robson to Sunderland, John McDowell and Alan Taylor to Norwich City and Mervyn Day, Tommy Taylor and Billy Jennings joined the very good Leyton Orient side Jimmy Bloomfield was building just up the road from Upton Park.

We received just over £630,000 from the sale of those players. That money was used to buy Ray Stewart from Dundee United and Stuart Pearson from Manchester United.

It was another summer of reflection, though I was very enthusiastic about the opening of our new £140,000 gymnasium at Chadwell Heath. I remembered as a young player how I had enjoyed playing indoor football during West Ham's training sessions at the Forest Gate roller-skating rink. We had later used the sports centre at Redbridge, and the atmosphere generated by playing in a confined area considerably enhanced the skill and technique of the players. When you have walls, the ball is never out of play, and the speed of the game encourages movement and sure touch. From the club's point of view, the new gym also gave us a facility that helped attract the best local schoolboys, and a couple of years later, in 1981, a lot of youngsters who learned the basics of the trade in that gym helped West Ham win the FA Youth Cup.

If our long-term future was looking rosier, the present was still a source of concern to me. We started the 1979–80 season lamentably, with just two wins from our first seven matches. We were never above fifth place and finished the season in seventh. It was another season of frustration for me, but my disappointment was eased by the success we enjoyed, first in the League Cup, and then much more dramatically in the FA Cup.

We beat Barnsley 5–1 over two legs in the second round of the League Cup and then met Southend in round three. Fourth Division they may have been, but they gave us a torrid time, holding out 1–1 and 0–0 before we finally won the second replay 5–1 at Upton Park. I particularly remember the first match, because I decided that the team that evening would include Paul Allen for the first time.

He had signed as a full professional the month before, on his seventeenth birthday. He was one of the most enthusiastic youngsters I'd worked with, and he became the holder of the record number of caps – twenty-three – for the England Youth team. Our early-season form in the Second Division was awful, and I felt we needed a little more devil in the middle of the field. All I asked him to do against Southend that night was hold his position in central midfield and win the ball for us. He was a revelation. He transformed us. Four days later he made his Second Division debut against Burnley at Upton Park. We won 2–1. It was only our third League win of the season. I kept him in the side for the rest of the season, and he was again an influential figure when we beat Sunderland 2–1 in a fourth-round replay in the League Cup.

For us, the moment of truth came against Nottingham Forest in round five. They were defending the League Cup and were also the European Cup holders. It was one of Brian Clough's best teams ... Shilton, Anderson, McGovern, Birtles, Robertson. Forest held us to a goalless draw at Upton Park and, although we were still goalless after ninety minutes of torrential rain in Nottingham, they beat us 3–0 in extra time, with goals from John O'Hare, Garry Birtles and Martin O'Neill.

But as that dream evaporated, so another was taking root. Three weeks after that Forest defeat, we visited West Bromwich Albion in the third round of the FA Cup. We had beaten Orient 4–0 on New Year's Day, and I can remember the players speculating afterwards about another good Cup run. West Brom, though, were a First Division side with a style of play that epitomized the thinking of their flamboyant manager, Ron Atkinson. We were completely overrun for long periods, but Phil Parkes produced one of the finest goalkeeping displays I've ever seen. Ron Atkinson laughed after the match: 'Ten out of ten? I'd give that boy twelve out of ten!' Stuart Pearson had scored for us against the run of play, and twenty seconds before the end Cyrille Regis equalized, although his goal had a suspicion of handball about it. So we escaped with a 1–1 draw, but Parkes was the man who had earned it for us. Months later, standing in the players' tunnel at Wembley, I looked over at him just before the teams walked out for the final. I thought: 'If it hadn't been for you, big man, we wouldn't be here now.'

We had to play the replay on a misty evening at Upton Park without the injured Billy Bonds, but we were far more controlled this time, winning 2–1 with goals from Geoff Pike and Trevor Brooking. We met our local rivals, Orient, in the fourth round at Brisbane Road. I was a little concerned about Bonds again, because he had received a serious head wound the week before, but he insisted on playing. He bound a protective bandage around his forehead, and when he led the players out he looked like Geronimo. He played like him too. I told the Press afterwards: 'The chief won his battle.' Our former centre half Tommy Taylor scored first from the penalty spot, but we fought back to win 3–2, Ray Stewart scoring two of our goals.

In round five we beat Swansea City, John Toshack's Second Division side, 2–0, Paul Allen and David Cross scoring within sixty seconds of each other late in the game at Upton Park. Fortune smiled on us in the quarter-final, when we were drawn at home to First Division Aston Villa. This time we were without Bonds because of injury, and Frank Lampard took over as captain. It was a tight, competitive match, decided in the last seconds by a penalty. Ray Stewart strode forward and, with his customary aplomb, drove the ball crisply beyond the reach of Jimmy Rimmer. I had noticed in training that, apart from the firmness and accuracy of his shooting, Ray had the ability to concentrate no matter how hard you tried to divert his attention. He had scored six penalties for us already that season, and this was perhaps his biggest test. He didn't let us down. That 1–0 victory secured an FA Cup semifinal meeting with Everton at Villa Park. Suddenly Wembley was just over the horizon.

By the time we met Everton in April, our chances of promotion from Division Two were remote. We won just one of our eight League games immediately before the semi-final and were in eighth place in the table. As the season had developed, the Cup competitions had increasingly dominated the thoughts of the players. In all we played seventeen Cup matches that season. Naturally, players want to win every game but, subconsciously, one competition invariably takes priority over another. The run of success we had in the League Cup gave them confidence, and the nearer we got to Wembley in the FA Cup, the more the players believed they would achieve their goal. It was our League form that suffered as a consequence.

A 47,000 crowd crammed into Villa Park for a hotly disputed semifinal. Brian Kidd scored for Everton with a penalty after forty-two minutes – he was later sent off. Stuart Pearson equalized in the sixty-eighth minute, and although Paul Allen scored late in the game the goal was disallowed because of offside. The replay at Elland Road four days later was just as frenetic. We lost our centre half Alvin Martin just before the game with tonsilitis. I had to rearrange the defence and put Bonds and Stewart together in the middle, moved Frank Lampard to right back, and brought in Paul Brush at left back. I knew we would miss Alvin's height and power in defence, and the big question was: would Bill and Ray between them be able to handle Bob Latchford, who was the England centre forward at the time and a formidable opponent in the air? Neither team scored in the first ninety minutes, but after four minutes of extra time Alan Devonshire scored a goal good enough to grace any semifinal. With seven minutes remaining, Latchford finally shook off the attentions of Bonds and Stewart and scored a superb goal to level the score. Then, as so often happens on these occasions, Frank Lampard emerged as a most unlikely goalscorer, clinching a Wembley place for West Ham and immediately celebrating with a little dance around one of the corner flags. It was a wonderful moment for me.

Six days after beating Everton, we faced Birmingham City in a Second Division match at Upton Park. We still had a faint, if unrealistic, chance of promotion, but a win for them would lift them into second place. It was a bitterly disputed match and, just after the interval with the score at 1–1, Billy Bonds clashed with the England defender Colin Todd. As they fell they kicked out at each other, and as they got to their feet they began exchanging blows. The referee, Alan Gunn, had no option but to send them both off for fighting. Billy, who was an experienced professional, was ashamed of himself afterwards. He should have known better. As he sat in the dressing room, the full implications of his actions began to dawn on him. The FA Cup Final – a big London 'derby' against Arsenal – was on 10 May, less than three weeks away. The Football Association suspension would almost certainly rule him out of the big day at Wembley. That was bad enough. The fact that Birmingham went on to beat us 2–1 finally killed off any hopes we still had of promotion.

West Ham appealed against the sending-off, and Bill and I went to the Football Association headquarters in Lancaster Gate, west London, for the hearing. The chairman of the appeal committee was Bert Millichip, who was also chairman of West Bromwich Albion, the team we had knocked out of the FA Cup in round three. By this time Bill had already served his automatic one-match ban, but a further suspension appeared inevitable. I looked at Mr Millichip, hoping that I might detect just a hint of sympathy. Bill's disciplinary record early in his career was, let's say, chequered, but in recent years he had made a sterling effort to improve his record. Mr Millichip agreed. The committee felt that the one-game suspension already served was enough. Bill was free to play at Wembley.

With Bill available and Alvin now fit again, I had a difficult choice to make when I came to select the team for the final. I needed both of them to play, so in the end it was a straight choice between the two full backs Frank Lampard and Paul Brush. Ray Stewart had established himself at right back, and I chose Frank to play at left back simply because of his experience. That was a quality we would need in abundance against a team of Arsenal's stature playing in their third consecutive FA Cup Final.

We enjoyed the build up for this big occasion probably more than the days before the 1975 Final against Fulham, when West Ham were clear favourites to win. This time

Arsenal were the favourites. There was little pressure on us. The night before the final we stayed in a hotel on the western outskirts of London, and the players sat in their rooms watching television. The big-match pundits were extolling the virtues of Arsenal, and Alan Mullery, who had played for Fulham against us in the 1975 Final, remarked that Bill and Alvin didn't compare as centre backs to the Arsenal pair of David O'Leary and Willie Young.

That day, too, Brian Clough, borrowing a famous line from Muhammad Ali, declared that Trevor Brooking 'stung like a butterfly'. Trevor and Bill, great pals, were sharing a room that night. Anyone who knew them well would know that such remarks were guaranteed to bring the best out of them. I was happy and relaxed. Five days before the final, we had beaten Charlton Athletic 4–1. The team performance was as good as the result suggests. Eddie Baily and I had watched Arsenal twice and had devised a plan that we believed would cause them a little concern. Arsenal had a well-balanced team and a rigid defensive pattern. I felt we needed to come up with something a little different, something that would confuse them and perhaps disturb their defensive organization. We were the underdogs, and I felt we could afford to gamble. I decided to play David Cross as a lone striker and drop his attacking partner, Stuart Pearson, into a withdrawn position in front of the midfield. You couldn't have experimented with such a tactical move in a Wembley Final with lesser players than Pearson and Cross. On the Wednesday before the game we had worked in training on the idea of dropping Pearson short, and it had looked promising.

Cross, who we had signed from West Bromwich Albion

for £180,000 – a club record at the time – in December 1977, was such a willing and resilient striker that we felt he had the strength to occupy both the Arsenal centre backs O'Leary and Young. In theory they should have been able to mark Dave successfully between them, but what they wouldn't be so sure about was how to mark Stuart Pearson. He played in the 'hole' between Dave and our midfield. Arsenal had to decide whether to mark him with a defender or a midfield player. Whatever they did it would disrupt their pattern. Alternatively, they could simply leave him free to play unhindered. It worked out exceptionally well for us. Arsenal never really solved the problem. We scored the only goal of the match after thirteen minutes, Trevor Brooking getting his head – just – to a cross from Pearson. At half-time I told the players in the dressing room that Arsenal might now push either Young or O'Leary forward to mark Pearson. If they did that, I told them, we would simply play the ball direct to David Cross, who would then be playing one-on-one against a solitary defender.

As it was, we held out in the second half, despite the magnificent contribution made by Liam Brady, who made chances that both Graham Rix and Frank Stapleton squandered.

At that time, Liam was in the process of establishing himself as one of the world's great players. I had enormous admiration for his technique, and when he later played for me at West Ham I realized just how much work he does for his teammates. He is not often given credit for the donkey-work. But that day back in 1980 it was his creative genius and that wonderful left foot that most concerned me. Paul Allen faced him on that side of the field and did a brilliant job for me. It was a memorable day for him, a fresh-faced youngster with no inhibitions at all. A lot of the media interest had been centred on him, because that day he became the youngest FA Cup Finalist in history, at 17 years 256 days. I think he must have tugged at the heart-strings of every mother in the nation as he came down the steps from Wembley's royal box with tears streaming down his face. He could have scored a goal, too, had Willie Young not felled him towards the end of the game. Every so often you come across an outstanding young player you can put in the first team – and keep there. More often than not you put a player in, pull them out after a few weeks, and bed them down gently. Paul got in and stayed, and nothing was going to shift him that season.

After the game the players climbed back into the coach and followed our escorting police motorcyclist into the West End for the club's celebration banquet. As we drove along Park Lane we passed the Arsenal coach, which had just come to a halt. Our police escort deliberately slowed down and gave them a mischevious wave. I didn't have the heart to do that. I remembered how I felt when we were relegated. It was, inevitably, one of those champagne evenings. Ernie Gregory, our long-serving goalkeeper coach, rarely drinks, but he had enjoyed a mouthful of champagne from a plastic cup in the dressing room after the match. Had you seen him that evening you would have imagined he had drunk three magnums of champagne. He spent most of the evening singing songs from the Boer War that he had learned during his army service. He was simply 'drunk' with the emotion of the occasion. Whenever I saw Trevor Brooking that evening he was in a stooped or crouched position. He was, of course, re-running his headed goal. He headed the ball only once that season – that day at Wembley.

Trevor was very tongue in cheek about his success. He, Billy Bonds and Frank Lampard had been the corner-stone of my teams at West Ham for about fifteen years, and they all shared the same quality – modesty. I've known players with lots of talent, but most of them liked to make sure you were aware of the fact. Brooking, Bonds and Lampard had talent, but never felt the need to shout about it.

I'd known Trevor since he came to West Ham as an academically gifted schoolboy. He and Frank were in my first youth group. He was to become one of West Ham's and England's most creative midfield players, but his development was slow. At one time Ron Greenwood was thinking of selling him to Southampton for £67,000. He didn't find the physical side of training easy, but he would never give in. If I gave the players a five-mile run, he would finish, no matter how long it took. I said to him more than once: 'OK Trev, the others have finished, you can stop now.' He'd glare at me and say: 'I'll finish.'

He had a competitive edge to his game that not too many people appreciated. But it was his determination to succeed that eventually made him such a great player. He was the classic improviser. Many players have one particular skill they call upon repeatedly in given situations. Trevor had two or three for most situations. That, plus his knack of playing the ball as late as possible, made him a very difficult man to mark successfully. He had a wonderful touch and great awareness. Most defenders would try to anticipate what he was going to do with the ball. Trevor would sense their positioning and their reaction and respond accordingly. He was one of the few players who was comfortable allowing the ball to run past him, and the way he used his body to shield the ball made him awkward to dispossess. Some coaches used to tell me that he wasn't very quick, but rarely, once he had swept past a defender, would he get caught by the same player. He had aggression, too, another facet of his game not widely acknowledged. Sometimes I'd say to Billy Bonds or Geoff Pike in training: 'Get after him and show him who's boss.' Trevor would just get more competitive in his attitude and hold them off. I'd say to them afterwards: 'You didn't do it.' And they'd say: 'We couldn't get near him.'

Trevor played more than 600 games for West Ham between 1967 and 1984. When he retired he had become one of football's most courteous ambassadors, a great example to young footballers and young people in general. His behaviour on and off the field was exemplary. If he had a failing it was his obsession with cards, a pastime to which he and Billy Bonds devoted countless hours. I remember standing behind him in the customs hall in Moscow airport on our way home from a European Cup Winners' Cup tie in Tbilisi in March 1981. Before we had entered the Soviet Union, each individual had filled in a form detailing our cash and traveller's cheques. On departing we filled in another form. Trevor's form revealed that he was leaving the country with more money than he brought in.

'Why?' asked the Russian customs officer.

'I won it playing cards,' explained Trevor.

I found Trevor immensely supportive throughout our years together at Upton Park. He was the type of person you could rely upon when the going was tough. When we were relegated to Division Two in 1978 he was at the height of his international career with England, and our demise provoked a lot of speculation in the newspapers about his future. It was inevitable in the circumstances, because his contract expired the season we went down. Would Second Division football, the newspapers were asking, wreck his international career?

The season had barely finished when he came to my office.

'Sorry to trouble you, John, but have you got a minute?' he asked. A minute was all it took. 'I just want you to know that I want to stay at West Ham and help get the team back into the First Division,' he said. 'I don't want to leave, but if for financial reasons the club has to sell me, I'll understand. OK?'

It was typical of Trevor. As everyone knows, he stayed at West Ham until he retired. Even today he pulls on a claret and blue shirt with number 10 on the back every week. He plays for a Sunday-morning team in Essex. They play in an old West Ham strip.

These days he's a successful businessman, and the knowledge he gathered during his years as a professional have made him a highly respected media commentator on the sport. He can be critical when necessary, but he's always constructive. Have I got anything bad to say about him? Well, he got cautioned by the referee at Burnley once!

If Trevor found the physical aspects of football a touch tiresome at times, Billy Bonds truly revelled in them. Physically, I'd have to set him apart from most of the other players I worked with. In terms of athleticism he was phenomenal. He won the pre-season cross-country races every year from my early days as a coach until he finally retired from playing at the age of 40. Within football circles his fitness was legendary and earned him, late in his career, an invitation to compete with other sportsmen in the *Superstars* series on television. He was a natural athlete, and often on a Friday before a hard match he would go for a long run. 'I don't feel right if I don't do that, John,' he used to say. He comes from south London and was born opposite the pierhead for the Woolwich ferry. He was always grateful for the encouragement he received from his parents. I remember a junior player once complaining about a long run in training. He turned to the young lad and said: 'If my father heard you say that he'd knock your block off.' Bill was very grateful for the living and the enjoyment he got from professional football.

I think his competitive instincts made him an inspiring captain, and he became very influential in the careers of younger players like Pat Holland, Geoff Pike and Paul Allen. For me, he was one of West Ham's all-time greats, and the only regret I have is that he never won the England cap he would have loved to present to his father. Ron Greenwood selected him for three England squads and put him on the bench for a World Cup tie against Italy in 1977. Probably the nearest he came to actually playing was four years later, when England played Brazil at Wembley. Alvin Martin made his international debut that day, and Ron had telephoned Bill and told him that he would definitely play. Sadly, in a match against Sheffield Wednesday the week before, Bill collided with Phil Parkes and broke a rib. Ron had bought Bill for West Ham from Charlton for £47,500 in 1967; Charlton asked for £50,000. Ron said he would give them the other £2,500 if Bill won an England cap. Charlton are still waiting.

Bill played 800 first team games for West Ham – a club record – between 1967 and 1986, and he scored a few goals too, especially when he was playing in midfield. People tend to dismiss him as a goalscorer, but he hit thirteen in 1973–4 – not a bad return for a midfield player.

As a player he was always first out of the dressing room after a match. His great joy remains his family. He's also a keen bird-watcher, and likes his garden and country walks – not pastimes you would readily associate with the buccaneering captain, head swathed in bandages, who never shirked a challenge. Today he's West Ham's youth team coach, and after a difficult first year in the job I believe he is getting to grips with it. He talks sense and is honest and constructive, and I think he will succeed as a coach.

Frank Lampard was another very special player. He made more than 600 appearances for the club between 1967 and 1985. He was totally dedicated to his career from the moment he first came to me as a 15-year-old. He had set his heart on a career as a footballer and became a manager's dream. If I dropped him he would never complain. He would listen to what you had to say and would then train by himself every afternoon, when the other players had finished, until he got back in the side. Whenever I left him out his response was: 'OK, John, I'll be back.' Like Billy, he was a prodigious trainer. When most of the other players were walking in for a shower after training, he would be lying on his back doing exercises. That's why his career lasted so long and was so successful. He was also a full back who thought about the game. Whichever player he marked, he made sure he knew all about their strengths and weaknesses. He worked particularly well on the left side when he and Graham Paddon were in the team together. They used to spend hours on the training pitch working out little free-kick routines. He underlined his fighting qualities by the way he came back from a badly broken leg he received against Sheffield United in April 1968. Today he runs his own businesses and also helps in the West Ham Centre of Excellence at Chadwell Heath. I know he is proud of his son Frank junior, who attends Brentwood School and is a very promising footballer. He has his father's appetite for the game.

TRANSFERS

The FA Cup Final victory was a tremendous personal boost to me. The manner of the win over Arsenal gave me enormous satisfaction and helped repair any damage my reputation had suffered following West Ham's relegation to the Second Division. At no time, though, did I sense any pressure from the board of directors; but deep inside me I realized that any manager of a relegated club was vulnerable. I had signed a five-year contract in the summer of 1975, a few weeks after our FA Cup Final win over Fulham and ten months after succeeding Ron Greenwood as team manager. Initially I stayed on my assistant manager's salary of £4,000 a year but, after that win at Wembley, the terms of my new contract offered a salary of £15,000 a year. Now that contract had expired. I was fortunate that we were negotiating new terms immediately after another Wembley success. I was also fortunate that our success coincided with Mr Len's first season as chairman.

I was therefore not only negotiating from a position of some strength but also knew that Mr Len and his directors appreciated the effort I had put into the 1979–80 season. I had an inkling of their future intentions that April when we had secured a place in the semifinals of the FA Cup and still had a faint chance of winning promotion from Division Two. On the first Saturday of the month, the week before we were to face Everton in the semifinal, we played our East London neighbours Orient at Upton Park. It was an important game, not just because of the approaching semifinal, but because I felt we could still have a significant say in the promotion race. I was in the dressing room with the players. It was one hour before the kick-off. For me, this was probably the most important hour of each week. It was essential that I sent the players on to the field in the right frame of mind.

This is the inner sanctum for a manager. He wants no interference in that hour. Only the team, coaching staff and physiotherapist were allowed in the dressing room in the hour before a match. Injured players and those not selected had to stay in the treatment room. I never allowed them to mill around in the dressing room while the team was preparing for a match. I liked my players to be relaxed when they came into the dressing room, but I wanted them bursting with enthusiasm and commitment when they went out on to the field. It was my job to wind them up gradually. If I felt that they peaked too soon, I would send them into the gym for a few minutes before the start of the match. I felt it was important to get them to concentrate on the task ahead. It's like the starting grid of a Grand Prix or the start line of the Olympic 100 metres final. I might spend a few minutes with individual players, or little groups of them, but I always held the big team meetings within forty-eight hours of a match. At that time they tended to be quick and concise. Experienced players like Bonds, Brooking, Lampard and Pearson didn't need long team-talks. They could size up opponents for themselves within five minutes of the kick-off. What I had to do in the hour before the kick-off was ensure that they were going to channel all their physical and mental powers into the match ahead. I didn't appreciate disturbances – and the board of directors realized that. Very occasionally the chairman might pop his head round the door, quickly say: 'All the best, boys,' and scurry away. On most Saturday afternoons, though, our privacy was respected.

But on this Saturday, against Orient, Mr Len knocked quietly on the dressing-room door thirty minutes before the kick-off.

'I'm sorry to trouble you, John, but if you get a moment before the match do you think you could nip up to the boardroom?' he asked rather pensively.

I was a bit abrupt with him – and that's probably putting it mildly.

'I'm sorry, Mr Len, I've got a job to do,' I said. 'If I get the chance I'll look in, otherwise I'll see you after the match.'

I think he left feeling rather deflated. 'OK, John,' he said. 'But it would be nice if we could see you before the game.'

Fifteen minutes before the kick-off the lads were coming to the boil. I sensed that our preparation was right. There were no last-minute problems. I dashed out of the dressing room, up the stairs and along the corridor to the boardroom. Mr Len was standing in the doorway with his arm across the door. He kept glancing inside at the other directors. 'Just a minute, John,' he said.

I wasn't in the mood for games. 'A minute is all I've got, Mr Len,' I said. Mr Len took one final look into the board-room.

'Sorry John. OK, you can come in now.'

Originally I thought they had wanted to introduce me to someone. But I knew everyone in the boardroom – all the

West Ham directors and a couple from Orient. Mr Len took a step forward.

'John,' he said, 'it's been a marvellous season already, and we felt we would like to show our appreciation now rather than wait to see what happens in the next few weeks.'

He handed me a limited-edition, solid-gold watch, inscribed on the back 'West Ham Utd FC. Well done, John. March 1980.' At that moment I didn't know quite what to say. I appreciated their kindness, but I knew I had treated the chairman somewhat shabbily in the dressing room doorway a few moments earlier.

'Mr Len, I'm sorry,' I said. 'I was busy downstairs. I thought you wanted me to meet someone. I didn't realize . . .'

That day we beat Orient 2–0. I went home and showed the watch to Yvonne. She knew about it: the club had asked her for suggestions.

It was the end of a perfect day for me. Those sort of gestures endear you to a club. That particular gesture, followed by our success in the FA Cup Final a few weeks later, suggested to me that I would have few problems when I came to negotiate a new contract during the summer. That, indeed, proved to be the case. The talks with Mr Len that summer were straightforward. They wanted to keep me at Upton Park. I wanted to stay. I signed a new contract for a further five years.

I felt in a strong position as manager. In the space of six months in 1979 I had paid a world-record fee for the Queen's Park Rangers goalkeeper Phil Parkes, £430,000 on the Dundee United defender Ray Stewart and £220,000 on the Manchester United and England striker Stuart Pearson. All three had played significant roles in West Ham's FA Cup success. Winning at Wembley had helped justify an outlay in the transfer market of more than £1.2 million on three players.

When we had been relegated in 1978 I set out to get back with a team good enough not just to win promotion but also to do well again in Division One. I had to make changes, and when I bought players I made sure they were of First Division quality. No one could question the status of Phil Parkes. He was not just of First Division quality, he was world class, as was reflected by the fee of £565,000.

I rarely offer an opinion on the transfer dealings of other managers, though some have said to me: 'They let him go cheaply' or 'I think they paid too much.' A player's transfer fee is largely relative to the needs of the buying club. If I need a player I am prepared to pay the asking price, providing the club has the money to spend. In the case of Parkes, I had been aware for some time that we needed a goalkeeper of his quality. Early in the 1978–9 season, Eddie Baily and I went to a match at Crystal Palace. Eddie sat next to the Queen's Park Rangers manager, Steve Burtenshaw, during the game. He was only joking when he said to Steve: 'Don't suppose you'd sell Parksy?'

Eddie had planted the seed. For the next couple of months I followed the QPR results, thinking that if they lost two or three games in succession they might decide to strengthen their team, and one way of financing that would be to capitalize on Phil Parkes on the transfer market. Eventually, after a series of phone calls, Rangers gave us permission to speak to Phil.

It was February 1979. I called Phil at his home in Woking-ham, and he asked Eddie and me to his house for talks. I have always preferred talking to players in their own homes, because they are far more relaxed and don't feel you are putting any pressure on them. We arrived in mid-afternoon, and after chatting for a couple of hours with him and his wife, Lavinia – I always like to involve the wives in transfer negotiations – we made him our offer. I sensed that he was feeling that this was perhaps the right time for him to move from Rangers. He was 29, had won an England cap five years earlier and I think felt that if his career was going to make any further progress he had to move to another club. I recall Lavinia saying that they enjoyed living where they were and did not want to move across to the east side of London. I said that they could remain living in the Woking-ham area. She then pointed out that Phil would struggle to reach our Chadwell Heath training headquarters by 10 o'clock every morning. She was right. It is a long way and, at that time of the day, a daunting daily journey.

'I'll tell you what,' I said. 'From now on we'll start training every day at 10.30.' If we want to be successful, I thought, we need the best players, and if we want to get the best players we have to understand their particular problems. From that week I moved training back to 10.30, give or take a few minutes, and that remained the start time until the day I left the club.

Phil and Lavinia wanted to discuss our offer in private. I asked them if they could give us a decision within a couple of hours. Eddie and I left their house, drove into town and had a steak. I think we sensed that he would sign for us.

'I'll get a bottle of wine for the Parkeses, just in case,' said Eddie.

A couple of hours later we went back to the house. We knocked on the door and within seconds Phil opened it. 'I'll sign,' were his first words. That evening, driving back along the M4, only four people knew the deal had been completed – Eddie and I and Mr and Mrs Parkes. I have always believed that a transfer should be negotiated and completed before the details are made public. That ensures there is no pressure on any of the parties involved. That apart, other managers have often told me – as they did on that occasion: 'You kept that one quiet, didn't you? I'd have liked to sign him.' That was probably one of the most satisfying and successful transfer deals I was involved in at West Ham. It required perseverance, and six months of patience, but it was worth the effort.

Initially, Phil travelled to and from the training ground by train – a four-hour return trip. Later, he, Alan Devonshire and Paul Goddard, who all lived in the same area, would sometimes drive across London together. Phil is a big, affable man and not once did he ever complain to me about the journey. He was a great professional, and the fact that he is still playing at the age of 39 speaks volumes for his character.

The Parkes transfer was a club record for West Ham as well as a world record for a goalkeeper at the time. But eighteen months later I established a new club record when I went back to QPR and paid £800,000 for Paul Goddard. Stuart Pearson was a wonderfully talented player but had been dogged by injuries during his three years at Upton Park, and I knew I would have to find a striker of similar quality to play alongside David Cross. I wanted a good team player, someone mobile to work around Cross and benefit from the openings he created with his height and aggression.

Paul Goddard was the ideal man. He emerged at Rangers

in the late seventies, one of the most exciting young strikers of the time. In the 1979–80 season, playing alongside another fine young striker, Clive Allen, Paul had scored sixteen goals. He was short in stature compared to Cross, but he had muscular legs and was full of running and enthusiasm. He was just 20 when I signed him, a little raw, perhaps, but with enormous potential. He was particularly effective when he had his back to goal. He could either turn sharply to shoot himself, or draw others players into the attack with his passing ability. I could envisage him establishing the same sort of goalscoring partnership that Cross had enjoyed with Pop Robson. These were the thoughts running through my head on the night before West Ham met Liverpool, the League champions, in the 1980 FA Charity Shield at Wembley. That evening I stayed with the team at the Hendon Hall hotel in north London to prepare for this most prestigious of pre-season friendly matches. When I arrived, the hotel receptionist handed me a telephone message asking if I would call Dennis Signy, a journalist and great personal friend with a soft spot for West Ham. As soon as I got to my room I called him at his home.

He asked if he could come and see me at the hotel because he had some news I might be interested to hear. He came straight over and told me that Rangers were prepared to sell Paul Goddard. I knew it had to be sound information, because at that time Dennis and the Rangers chairman, Jim Gregory, were close friends. These days you are more likely to get that sort of information from a player's agent. I had a lot of calls from agents in my later years at West Ham asking if I was interested in buying players. My answer to these people followed the same pattern. 'Do you have the permission of the player's club to offer him for sale?' was always my first question. I then usually told the agent that if I was interested I'd contact the club involved myself.

That is exactly what I did that evening in Hendon. The first call, from my hotel room, was to the Rangers manager, Tommy Docherty. We talked for a few minutes and then Tom passed me to his chairman. I asked him the fee. Mr Gregory told me it would be £800,000, and I agreed to pay that immediately. As we were due to face Liverpool at Wembley the following day, there was not a lot else I could do at that particular moment. Tommy asked me to speak to Jim Gregory on Sunday to discuss how we pay the fee. Liverpool beat us 1–0 in the Charity Shield, but the following day I put that disappointment behind me when I called Mr Gregory. He is a very astute and articulate businessman, and negotiating with him was an education. It took me until four in the afternoon to settle the terms of the payment. The fee, as agreed with QPR, was £800,000. We made a down payment, with the remainder paid over an agreed period. Mr Gregory was obviously an expert. Two months earlier, he had sold Clive Allen to Arsenal for £1.25 million. But for West Ham, Paul Goddard's fee was a new club record.

It transpired that Crystal Palace were also interested in signing him, so at 4 o'clock that Sunday afternoon Eddie and I drove through west London to Paul Goddard's house. Paul had played in the QPR side with Phil Parkes, who spoke in glowing terms of the young man's character and attitude. He was called 'Sarge' by his team mates at Rangers, because he had served in the Boys' Brigade. His father had also been in the Salvation Army. I have always felt it important to establish the character of a player before signing him, but there is a danger in looking for perfection. You have to remember when signing a player that, whatever his character, he is the same man as the one you looked at and liked on the playing field. If there's something about him that causes you some doubt, you have to ask yourself whether you can control that aspect of his personality. If you don't think you can control it, you don't buy him. I can remember only one instance when I decided against buying a player because of a weakness in his character. I'm not the sort of manager that makes extensive phone calls to establish a player's personality. I remember what I hear, what other managers say about players during conversations, and I store that away for future reference. But I recognize that a good team is made up of all sorts of characters. A lad who likes a drink after a game can lead the most disciplined life from Monday to Saturday. In Paul Goddard's case I had no doubts. Not only was he a goalscorer of outstanding potential, but he was also a player of excellent character. That was obvious within a few minutes of sitting down in his lounge with him and his wife, Debbie. They struck me as a very sensible couple.

Paul was interested in more than just the terms of his contract. He wanted to know how we played at West Ham, what we thought about the game and how we envisaged his role within the team. He wanted to spend that evening thinking it over.

Eddie and I drove back across London. Next morning Paul called me and said he would sign. Four days after he signed, he made his debut against Luton Town at Upton Park. It was the opening day of the 1980–81 season. We lost 2–1, and I had to replace Paul with substitute Frank Lampard after fifty-eight minutes because of a groin strain.

Again, it was a very satisfactory transfer deal, completed with the minimum of fuss and publicity. I have always made it a rule never to encourage or in any way be part of the transfer speculation that seems to be the hard currency of many tabloid newspapers these days. At West Ham I preferred to keep such business private until the club was in a position to make a formal announcement. If I was on transfer business, going to watch or talk to a player, I would prefer to travel quietly and arrive unseen. Perhaps I was fortunate in some respects, because I have never been one of the high-profile managers whose regular appearances on television or in the newspapers guarantees instant recognition. None the less, sometimes I was recognized, and one such instance, shortly before I signed Goddard, revealed an uncanny chain of occurrences dating back to my father's childhood in the village of Kirriemuir in Scotland. At the end of the previous season, before the FA Cup Final against Arsenal, Eddie Baily and I wanted to go to Dundee to watch a striker called Ian Ferguson. At this time West Ham were seventh in the table and had no chance of winning promotion in the remaining games, so we chose to fly to Edinburgh airport early on a Saturday morning.

At the airport we were due to collect a hired car. I remember standing in the airport concourse looking for the signs that might direct us to the hire company. We must have looked bewildered, because a stranger emerged from the crowd, tapped me on the arm and said: 'Can I help you, Mr Lyall?' I was never fanatical about travelling incognito to watch a player, but at that moment it was irritating to know I had been spotted. Eddie, who can be a little more blunt than me, told the gentleman in a pin-striped suit that we were not in need of assistance. I was a little more diplomatic and explained that we were looking for a car-hire company. The gentleman insisted that he be allowed to lead us to the car-hire firm. To be honest, there was something about his manner and bearing that was quite impressive. Eddie and I looked at each other and then followed him. As we walked along together, he turned to me and said: 'Perhaps I should introduce myself. I know your uncle. My cattle are sold to his butcher's shop in Kirriemuir. I am Lord Lyell.'

Naturally, when he invited us back to his home, just outside my late father's village of Kirriemuir, we had to accept. Eddie and I climbed into our car and followed him. We drove through Kirriemuir, parts of which I remembered from my childhood, and out into the country again before turning into an imposing driveway that wound through a forest.

'Where's he taking us?' said Eddie, who was feeling a little uncomfortable about the whole venture.

Finally, the cars came to a halt in front of Kinnordy House, the stately home of Charles Lyell, the third baron of Kinnordy. He ushered us inside, where we were introduced to his mother and drank sherry. We sat and talked. Although our surnames were spelled differently, our families came from the same part of Scotland, and we speculated about the possibility of some distant relationship.

His family had a military background, and his father, killed in action in 1943, was awarded the Victoria Cross. Charles Lyell was educated at Eton and Oxford and had himself served as an officer in the Scots Guards. Today he is Parliamentary Under-Secretary of State in the Northern Ireland Office and in later years, when West Ham played pre-season friendly matches in Scotland, I would invite him to join us for dinner. I remember before one match against Dundee United asking one of the West Ham directors, Mr Will, if he would mind sitting with a friend of mine at dinner and acting as host. Mr Will looked a bit perplexed but I reassured him.

'He's a nice man, Mr Will,' I said. 'You'll be impressed.'

Mr Will had no idea who he would be dining with, and when Lord Lyell arrived at the hotel, I introduced them.

'Mr Will,' I said. 'This is Lord Lyell.'

Mr Will looked astonished. 'Pardon?' he said. 'Lord who?'

During my first encounter with Lord Lyell, he explained that he had followed my career with some interest over the years. He knew my father's family came from the village of Kirriemuir, but what had really stirred his interest was an extraordinary coincidence that went back more than twenty years. As an 18-year-old footballer at West Ham, I had my first knee operation in a London hospital. As I was wheeled out of the operating theatre, the next patient to come in was Lord Lyell, who was having surgery to repair a leg broken in a skiing accident. Neither of us would have known anything of the coincidence had it not been for the anaesthetist in the hospital that day. With Lord Lyell stretched out before him, waiting to go under, he looked at his clipboard and said: 'That's amazing. The patient before you was a young foot-baller called Lyall.'

From that day, Lord Lyell followed my career. On the day I met him for the first time, we left his stately home and he, Eddie and I drove on to Dundee where we watched the match and ate pies on the terraces.

I spent a lot of my time at West Ham watching Scottish

matches and, like Eddie Baily, I admired the qualities of Scottish players. When Eddie was assistant to Bill Nicholson at Tottenham, they built their best teams around Scotsmen like Bill Brown, Dave Mackay, John White, Alan Gilzean and Jimmy Robertson. The best of the Scots players combined dash, gallantry and flair with resilience and fortitude. I signed several for West Ham, and all had one thing in common – they never shirked a challenge. Not all of them were totally successful at Upton Park, but I like to think that they all left better players.

Neil Orr certainly came into that category. The son of former Scotland international Tommy Orr, West Ham signed him from Morton for £325,000 in January 1982. A youngster of potential, he developed enormously during his five years at Upton Park, but competition for places meant that he couldn't secure a regular first-team spot. Eventually, he decided that he wanted to move back to Scotland, and we agreed a fee with Hibernian. The transfer forms hadn't been signed when the Hibs manager, Alex Miller, called me at Upton Park on a Friday morning and told me that he wanted Neil to make his debut next day. Could we get the player and the forms to Scotland in time? That afternoon I flew to Edinburgh with Neil and our club secretary, Tom Finn. We checked into a hotel, and Tom's first task was to ensure that the hotel secretarial service could provide us with a typist to fill out the transfer forms. Eventually, after all the details of the deal had been finalized, we called down to the reception desk to ask for the typist. Bad news – the typist had finished work and gone home. Without the typist there were no forms, and without the forms Neil Orr couldn't play for Hibs the next day.

At this point I remembered the days in the office at West Ham, when I had painstakingly learned to type with two fingers.

'Bring me a typewriter,' I said. 'I'll have a go.' The problem was that the hotel gave me an electric typewriter. I had never used one before. The slightest touch of a key produced a blur of print on the forms. It took a dozen attempts to complete the financial agreement in something approaching an acceptable fashion. My typing was just about good enough, and Neil made his debut for Hibs the following day.

I sometimes wonder when reading about a 'transfer hitch' in the newspapers exactly what went wrong to bring about the problem. Sometimes you learn the truth, sometimes you don't. No one ever knew, for instance, that my bid to persuade François van der Elst to play for West Ham could have been wrecked by thirty-nine bursts in the plumbing system at the house I was hoping he would choose to live in during his stay in England. That was one of my few transfer deals in which an agent was involved. I first learned of François's availability when I received a call from Dennis Roach, a licensed UEFA agent who was later to be instrumental in the transfers of Glenn Hoddle from Tottenham to Monaco and Chris Waddle from Tottenham to Marseille. François was playing for New York Cosmos at the time, and Dennis told me that he wanted to play in England. He didn't have to try too hard to sell him to me. I remembered François well from our defeat by Anderlecht in the European Cup Winners' Cup Final in 1976. He had been devastating against us that night, running at our defence with pace and diligence. I told Dennis I would like to sign him. The fee was going to be around £450,000, and we agreed that it would be best for all concerned if he had a week's trial with us first. He had been playing American soccer and in terms of commitment that is vastly different from the English First Division.

He came and worked hard with us for a week at Chadwell Heath. Technically, he was a superb player. The contractual negotiations with him were simple. I then had to agree a fee with the Cosmos, who were owned by Warner Brothers. I went to their offices in Kensington and we agreed to pay £450,000. François still had his house in Belgium, but obviously we had to find him somewhere to live near to Upton Park. At that time the club owned a house at Shenfield in Essex, where Stuart Pearson had been the previous occupant. François signed for us on Christmas Eve 1981, and early in the New Year I drove him, his wife and their two children from their hotel in Epping through the Essex countryside to Shenfield. They liked the area and felt that it was not that different from where they lived in Belgium. By the time we arrived at the empty house in Shenfield it was dusk. I walked to the front door with the van der Elst family behind me, and, as I put the key in the door, I thought I could hear running water. I opened the door and as I walked down the hallway the sound of running water grew louder. François and his family were right behind me. I opened the door of the kitchen, took one step inside, and immediately got a boot full of water.

'I think we've got a little problem here, François,' I said. My embarrassment was complete when we walked into the lounge – all thirty-five feet of it was under four inches of water.

'Don't worry, François, a minor hitch,' I said as I

shepherded them back out to the car. Because I couldn't use the lights in the house, I took a torch from the car, went back through the front door and climbed up the stairs. Somewhat gingerly, I opened the bathroom door – and was showered. There was a hole in the ceiling and the water was pouring through.

François and his family were very understanding as I drove them back to their hotel in Epping. I assured him that all would be well. And it was, eventually. It had been a cold winter, and the house had been empty for a long time with no heating. In all, there were thirty-nine bursts in the plumbing system; I remember because each was detailed on the bill when it arrived from the plumber. I also remember Yvonne, Murray and me going back to Shenfield to help clean the house. Eventually it was ready and François and his family moved in. A more pretentious individual might have pulled out of the deal.

Sadly, I didn't even get as far as showing property to Brian Greenhoff, the Manchester United and England midfield player or defender. I was looking for a right back and was delighted eventually to sign Ray Stewart from Dundee United. But Greenhoff was an option. Ron Greenwood was the England manager at the time, and at a dinner in London he happened to mention to me how impressed he had been with Brian in his squad. I stored that information away and a few weeks later was talking with the Manchester United manager, Dave Sexton, an old colleague of mine from my playing days at West Ham. I asked him about QPR's right back, Dave Clement, who I was interested in. Dave Sexton had been manager at Rangers and knew all there was to know about Clement. During the course of the conversation

I also asked if there was any likelihood of United selling Greenhoff, who, apart from playing at right back, could play in the centre of the defence or in midfield. Brian wasn't in the United team at the time, and Dave gave me permission to talk to him. When I called Brian he was out playing golf, but I arranged to call back at six in the evening. I warned Eddie Baily that we might be doing some transfer business that night. He was thrilled, because he loves the chase and excitement of a big transfer.

'One problem,' I told him. 'My car's being serviced.'

'No problem,' said Eddie. 'We'll take mine.' At six o'clock I spoke to Brian Greenhoff, and although he wasn't sure that he wanted to live in the London area he said that he would like to talk to us. It was up to us, then, to try to persuade him. Eddie drove to Upton Park to collect me in his rather elderly Cortina. It was a foul night and it took hours to get to Brian's beautiful house on the outskirts of Manchester. When we pulled up on his drive it was nearly midnight, and I was a little apprehensive when I knocked on the door. I needn't have been. Brian and his wife were very understanding and we sat and talked. He asked for time to think about it. A few days later he came to London simply to see if he and his wife felt they could live in or near the city. They decided that it wasn't the place to raise a family. I was disappointed, because he was a good player. He later signed for Leeds United.

We faced similar problems when we tried to sign David Cross. He wasn't sure that he wanted to live in London either. But, with his transfer, that was merely the final hurdle in a saga that stretched back more than four years. Ron Greenwood had originally tried to sign Dave from Norwich

City in November 1973. In fact, he wanted to sign both Dave and the Norwich winger Graham Paddon. A few weeks earlier, a lad called Jim Bone had come down from Scotland and joined Norwich. He was an instant hit, and his goalscoring exploits generated all sorts of headlines in the papers. Typically, Ron said to me one day: 'Let's go and have a look at this chap.' So we went to watch Jim Bone play at Carrow Road, and, although he did well, David Cross was the player that caught the eye.

His energy, attitude and enthusiasm were incredible. He ran himself into the ground that night. Ron and I were both impressed and he decided to try and buy both Cross and Paddon. The day he tried to put the deal in motion, Dave signed for Coventry for £150,000. Ron went ahead and signed Paddon, but I know he was disappointed to miss Cross. Three years later, Coventry decided to sell Dave. Ron tried to sign him again then, but he didn't want to live in London. He preferred to stay in the Midlands, and he signed for West Bromwich Albion for £120,000. So we had missed him twice. But a year later, when Cyrille Regis burst on the scene, Albion decided to sell Dave. We tried again for him, but I remember that he didn't want to live in London. I agreed a fee of £180,000 with Albion – a club record at the time for West Ham – and then I spoke to Dave. I told him we had been trying to sign him for years and that we were aware of his reluctance to move to London. In those circumstances, I said, the best thing for us to do was to show him London and the traffic problems at their worst. He came to Upton Park and I remember driving from the ground to my house with him during the evening rush-hour. Throughout the drive home I was thinking: 'Will he accept that he has to live with this traffic if he comes here?' When I got to my house I asked him what he thought.

'Not as bad as I imagined,' was his reply. He then drove home and later that evening called my house. I was out, so he spoke to Yvonne.

'Tell John I'll sign,' he said.

I was delighted. He was a player who gave me everything from the moment of his debut for us against his old club, WBA, in December 1977. His goals played a crucial role in helping us climb out of Division Two and reach the 1980 FA Cup Final. He made a lot of friends at West Ham with his charm and wit, and he revealed a remarkably deep general knowledge during the quizzes the players used to organize for long coach trips.

He always struck me as a very content man, though there was what he considered a glaring omission from his playing career. I was chatting to him during pre-season training in the summer of 1980, and he told me that the one big regret of his career was that he had never scored twenty goals in a season. He had never before gone beyond seventeen. He seemed to start well with plenty of goals, he said, but he couldn't maintain that form throughout the nine months of a season. Well, the beginning of that season, 1980–81, was to prove no different from any of the others. By the end of October he had scored sixteen goals.

'You're going to get twenty goals this season, Crossie,' I told him.

'Never,' he replied.

'I'll tell you what, Crossie. I'll give you £5 for every goal you get over twenty. And you give me £5 for every goal under twenty. It's a good bet for you.'

He didn't need telling twice. By March we were ten points clear at the top of Division Two, and Dave had scored a total of twenty-eight goals.

We clinched the Second Division title that season with a 2–0 home win over Bristol Rovers on 4 April. Dave didn't score; in fact, it was the third consecutive match in which he hadn't scored. But I was in a jubilant mood, quite naturally. Our next match was away to Grimsby and by this time he had scored twenty-nine goals. I told him I would give him £10 for every goal from thirty upwards, but if he stuck on twenty-nine he would have to give me £20. He agreed. The match attracted Grimsby's biggest gate of the season – nearly 18,000. It had been raining heavily and the pitch was deplorable. I sat in the stand next to one of the directors, Brian Cearns.

After fifteen minutes, Phil Parkes hit a long clearance down the middle. Dave chased it, muscled his way past defenders, and drove the ball into the net. Just my luck, I thought. Instinctively I felt for my wallet, knowing that I would have to present him with his £10 in the dressing room otherwise I would be the butt of Crossie's wicked humour. I was still searching through my pockets for the wallet when he scored a second goal. At this point I realized I had no wallet and no money with me. I turned to Brian Cearns.

'I'm sorry, Brian, but I've come out without any money, and those two goals have just cost me £20.'

Brian kindly fished around in his pocket and pulled out £20. I thought that was the end of it. We were leading 3–1 with four minutes to go, when he completed his hat-trick. Without looking at me, Brian handed over another £10.

'I hope he doesn't score any more,' he said.

I was feeling a bit uncomfortable at this point and was praying for the final whistle when ... he scored his fourth goal.

He tried hard not to smile at me when I walked into the dressing room afterwards. I gave him his £40. He stood up. Beneath the glistening film of sweat and mud on his face, he was smiling.

'Thanks John,' he said. Then he took £20 and walked round the dressing room, giving £5 to each of the four players who had provided the four passes from which he had scored. He was a nice guy, Crossie.

THE CHAMPIONSHIP SEASON

As a player, David Cross wasn't in the traditional West Ham mould when we first signed him. He was hard and uncompromising, but over the years his touch and his positioning improved significantly. I knew instinctively that he and Paul Goddard, a West Ham natural with a sure touch and crisp passing ability, would form a sound attacking partnership. I was proved to be correct. In 1980–81, the first season they played together, they shared fifty-six goals. Their prowess in the opposition's penalty areas was one of the major factors in what I consider to be the most satisfying season in my managerial reign at West Ham.

It was not the only factor, though. Phil Parkes was at the peak of his career, Ray Stewart had settled in impressively at right back and won his first Scotland cap, Alvin Martin was developing rapidly as a centre half of quality and, of course, Billy Bonds, Frank Lampard and Trevor Brooking provided the team with a hard core and that essential balance of flair and aggression. So, I had high hopes of finally regaining our First Division status in 1980–81. It was to prove a rewarding and traumatic season.

AUGUST

As the FA Cup winners, West Ham faced the League Champions, Liverpool, in the Charity Shield at Wembley. We lost 1–0, Terry McDermott scoring the goal after eighteen minutes, but we played well enough and I was not too disappointed. The compensation that weekend, of course, was the signing of Goddard from Queen's Park Rangers. With him in the side, I thought we now had a team capable of sustaining a season-long challenge for promotion. A crowd of 28,000 watched our opening match against Luton at Upton Park. We paraded the FA Cup, Goddard made an indifferent debut, and we lost 2–1. It wasn't the start I had been looking for.

Back at Chadwell Heath on Monday morning I stressed to the team that the FA Cup Final, and all the glory that that involved, was now a thing of the past. We had to forget about it. The only match that mattered now was the next one, and that was away to Bristol City. In fact, the next two games were away. We had received a great deal of flattering publicity in the previous few months, but I told the players that we could take nothing for granted. We had to work for our success. The next two away matches were going to be difficult. I didn't want another defeat gnawing at their confidence. We had to be realistic and resolute and, at the very least, remain undefeated. We went to Bristol and secured a 1–1 draw, and then, in another determined performance, took a point away from Preston with a goalless draw. They may not have been pretty matches, but at least we had stabilized a little. Then, in our second home game of the season, the work on the training ground suddenly began to produce results. We beat Notts County 4–0, Goddard scoring twice, with Cross and Ray Stewart getting the others. That result, plus a 2–0 win at Burnley in the first leg of the second round of the League Cup, meant that I finished the month in a more buoyant mood than I started it.

SEPTEMBER

This was a brilliant month for us in the Second Division. We won four consecutive matches, scoring nine goals and conceding three. The Cross–Goddard partnership was beginning to look really effective. They scored a goal apiece against Shrewsbury and a goal apiece against Cambridge. That apart, Goddard scored again in the 4–0 second-leg win over Burnley in the League Cup, and Cross hit both West Ham's goals in the 2–1 win over Charlton Athletic in the third round. By the end of the month we were second in Division Two and through to round four of the League Cup.

I was particularly delighted for Goddard. So impressive had his early season form been that he was called into the England Under-21 side for the first time. He scored twice in the 3–0 win over Norway at Southampton.

But the success we enjoyed on the domestic front was completely overshadowed by the incidents on the terraces that accompanied the club's return to Europe after an absence of five years. Having beaten Arsenal at Wembley the previous May, we qualified to play in the European Cup Winners' Cup, and our first-round opponents were Castilla of Spain. They were a good side playing in the Spanish Second Division. They acted as a nursery club for the mighty Real

above On opposite sides, but still great pals – me with one of the world's outstanding players, Bobby Moore, after the 1975 FA Cup Final against Fulham.

below My first trophy, the FA Cup, and it was a privilege to share the moment with Ron Greenwood.

I liked my teams to play with some style, and I also appreciated the style of the West Ham fans. Over the years I established a great rapport with the Upton Park crowd.

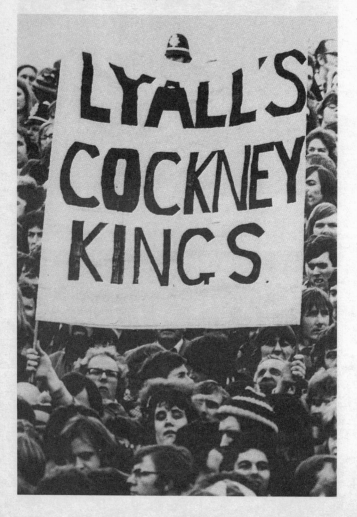

above The family day – the children's Christmas party at Chadwell Heath. We all helped make it a special occasion for the wives and children.

below It was always a great pleasure to coach the kids in the gym at Chadwell Heath. The concentration on their faces was a reward in itself.

Actions speak louder than words. The coach's stage is a football field and, just like an actor, the coach must be prepared to give a performance. I didn't always win Oscars for my performances – but I always followed the golden rule handed to me by Ron Greenwood.

above He didn't often head the ball, but when he did it was usually a bit special. Trevor Brooking's winning goal against Arsenal in the 1980 FA Cup Final at Wembley.

below Newham's Lady Mayor, Councillor Mrs Marjorie Helps, having a quiet word with me at the civic reception after the 1980 FA Cup Final.

above Rubbing shoulders with the best – a proud moment as Liverpool manager Bob Paisley and I lead out our teams before the 1981 League Cup Final.

below The dispute with referee Clive Thomas immediately after the 1981 League Cup Final at Wembley – David Cross intervenes at a highly charged moment.

above The banner says it all – done the West Ham way. Winning the Second Division Championship remains one of my most cherished memories.
below Loftus Road with QPR manager Jim Smith when our cup game was interrupted by the crowd spilling on to the pitch.

Madrid and shared their spectacular Bernabeu Stadium, with a capacity of 100,000. Although drawn to play in Madrid in the first leg, there was some confusion over the venue. Real Madrid were drawn at home against the Irish champions, Limerick, in the first leg, and it was thought that their match would take priority. If that were the case, West Ham would stage the first leg at Upton Park. Finally, UEFA decreed that Castilla would indeed stage the home leg first in Madrid, and so we travelled to play them on 17 September. The match itself was a thrilling affair of swaying fortunes, with Cross putting West Ham in front after eighteen minutes. The Spanish players had excellent technique and kept their composure during a compelling second half in which they scored three goals. We lost 3–1 – but the match was not all we lost.

The club's reputation suffered appalling damage as a result of the disturbances on the terraces that night. There were several hundred West Ham supporters in a crowd of 40,000, and the vast majority behaved impeccably. After the game, I was told that a few, a very few, by their disturbing and disorderly conduct, disgraced themselves and the club.

I saw little of what happened on the terraces that night. I was sitting in the dug-out, concentrating on the game, and the disturbances were behind me and to my right. I was aware that something amiss had occurred when a long troop of policemen, two abreast, marched across the face of the dug-out. I remember hearing a police chief blow a whistle. His men disappeared on to the terraces and were back on the pitch within five minutes. What compounded the problem for the club were incidents outside the stadium after the game. One West Ham supporter was hit by a motor coach and later died in hospital, a sad and tragic accident. After the game, the Press inevitably concentrated on the violence inside and outside the ground. They wanted to know my feelings, but in truth there wasn't a lot I could tell them. I was aware of the problems but hadn't seen them. I was more concerned with the effect the disturbances had on the team. I have no doubt that our play was disrupted that night by what was happening on the terraces.

The next day, of course, 'hooligan' headlines blazed from every newspaper. It was a growing problem throughout Europe. A riot by Sheffield Wednesday fans earlier in the month at Oldham had reduced Jack Charlton to tears. The Football Association had just formed a committee to deal with the problem of crowd disturbances. Now West Ham were suddenly thrust into the forefront of the fight against hooliganism. I thought then, and still do, that football hooliganism was definitely a symptom of the times. The game reflects the daily life of the country. Hooliganism is not confined to football terraces. It happens in pubs, clubs, dance halls, discos and on the streets of some of our quietest country towns.

It was established that 95 per cent of West Ham fans that night behaved as they always do, very well. The other five per cent spoiled the occasion for the majority. After the match our commercial manager, Brian Blower, remained in Madrid to liaise with police and ascertain the true facts. The information he gathered from official sources showed earlier reports to be grossly exaggerated. There were two arrests (both away from the ground), no interference with the match or match officials, and no damage to the stadium. Five supporters were detained for a short period during the game. Two fans arrested and five detained in a crowd of 40,000 – is that a good or a bad statistic? One arrest, or one injury, is one too many at a football match, but we have to keep statistics in perspective. I imagine that a police chief in any town with a 40,000 population would consider it a relatively quiet night if Saturday passed with only two arrests. That, of course, does not excuse the behaviour of the West Ham fans who were involved in the trouble that night. It is because of people like them that the game I love is now wrestling with the biggest single problem it has faced. I think the Government and the football authorities have to consider all and every means to solve the hooligan problem. The question of issuing identity cards requires careful study. We need to introduce a system in football that is practical and acceptable to all parties. Identity cards would be worthwhile if we could be sure that they would function properly at the turnstiles on a Saturday afternoon. The experts in these situations are football club administrators, and they are not sure. My overall feeling on the subject, though, is that if society took proper care in raising children the problem would not exist. But it does, and, for football's sake, we have to find a solution that can help us control the problem inside and outside grounds.

UEFA's solution on that occasion was more concerned with the short term – the second leg, due to be played at Upton Park on 1 October. A week after the match in Madrid, the club was fined £7,700 and ordered to play the second leg on a ground at least 300 kilometres (186 miles) from Upton Park. They further ordered that if we beat Castilla on aggregate, we would have to play our home leg in the second round away from Upton Park. UEFA gave us forty-eight hours to appeal and three days to find an alternative ground on which to stage the return leg against Castilla. Initially, we estimated that the punishment would cost the club around £30,000 in revenue. The board discussed the UEFA decision and decided to appeal. Meanwhile, we arranged to play the second leg at Roker Park, Sunderland.

At the end of the month I flew to Zurich to appear before the UEFA appeals board with Brian Blower and two club directors, Jack Petchey and Brian Cearns. We presented them with a dossier of facts, the results of the club's own exhaustive investigations into what had happened. UEFA listened sympathetically and, at the end of the hearing, announced they were lifting the fine imposed on the club and allowing us to play the second leg behind closed doors at Upton Park. Furthermore, if we progressed to the second round we would be allowed to stage the home leg at Upton Park.

OCTOBER

The relief I originally felt at the end of the UEFA hearing began to evaporate as I puzzled over how to prepare my team for a European game in an empty stadium. We were trailing 3–1 from the first leg, and normally in those circumstances the atmosphere generated by a packed house at Upton Park plays a vital role in fuelling the players. This time there would be no atmosphere.

I decided to play two full-scale practice matches at Chadwell Heath. In both games I asked the reserve lads to tackle, chase and harry the first-team players as if it was a competitive match. I wanted them to get some idea of what it was going to be like playing a fiercely competitive match without an audience. I geared up the training routines so that they were more competitive than usual. I had the added problem of a worry over the fitness of Trevor Brooking. He was troubled by a deep-seated groin strain and had been advised to rest for three weeks. I excused him from the competitive training, and he had a fitness test on the morning of the match and felt he could survive for the ninety minutes.

It was a unique occasion in the history of West Ham. Standing outside the ground, it was impossible to tell that a major European tie was about to be played. The official attendance that night is recorded as 262. That figure included players, match officials, administration staff and media men who, of course, christened the occasion 'The Ghost Match'. It was certainly eerie in the dressing rooms before the game. Usually, before a big match you can hear the murmur of the crowd outside and the fans clicking through the turnstiles. On this occasion there was only an inhibiting silence, which made the task of preparing the players more difficult than usual. The referee, the Dutchman Jan Keizer, visited both dressing rooms and said that he would treat the game no differently from any other game. He acknowledged that it would be difficult for both teams, but he wanted the job done properly. It was difficult for him, too, but he handled the game well. He had a distinguished career as a referee, and I later got to know him well.

When he blew his whistle to start the game, the noise echoed round the ground. From above me high in the stand, I – and probably everyone else in East Ham – could hear Eddie Baily shout: 'Get stuck into them.' By the end of the match he had lost his voice. Geoff Pike hit a glorious 25-yard shot after just nineteen minutes to put us ahead. Our plan was to drive a lot of high passes into Cross, and after thirty minutes he got his head to a Brooking free kick to put us level on aggregate. Then Cross set up a chance for Goddard to score our third just before the interval. In the second half the Spaniards fought back, just as they had done in the first leg. Their captain, Miguel Bernal, scored with a superb long-range shot after fifty-six minutes, and that took the game into extra time. By now even the ball boys, who were chasing around deserted terraces to retrieve the ball, were exhausted. But not Cross. He scored twice in extra time to complete his hat-trick, secure a 6–4 aggregate win and take West Ham into the second round.

I hoped that our next trip into Europe would be less eventful. We were drawn to meet Politechnica Timisoara of Romania, playing in European competition for only the second time. Little was known about them except that they had beaten Celtic in the first round. The score against Celtic was level 2–2 over two legs, but the Romanians went through on the away-goals rule. One of my first calls was to Billy McNeill, the Celtic manager, who was immensely helpful. He told me of the Romanians' spirited display in Timisoara, when three players were sent off and five cautioned. I was also fortunate in that just before our first leg, England played a World Cup tie against Romania in Bucharest, losing 2–1. My assistant, Eddie Baily, sometimes joined Ron Greenwood, then England manager, on occasional scouting trips. He went to Bucharest with the England party.

He saw England's World Cup defeat and, the day before, he had also watched the Under-21 side lose 4–0 to the Romanians. A number of the Timisoara players had been involved in those two games, and the big bonus for us was that he was also able to watch Timisoara lose 2–1 to the Yugoslav side OFK Belgrade in a friendly match. He came back full of information and, like Billy McNeill, stressed the level of commitment the Romanians took in every match. So, we were well prepared.

They were, indeed, a talented side, but we played brilliantly in front of a 27,000 crowd. Billy Bonds headed in a Ray Stewart free kick after twenty-four minutes, and six minutes later we were 3–0 ahead after Goddard and Stewart (with a penalty) had added further goals. Finally, a goal from David Cross in the eighty-third minute meant that we would travel to Romania defending a comfortable 4–0 lead.

Our form in the Second Division remained encouraging. We were unbeaten throughout October, stretching our undefeated run of League games to twelve. At the end of the month we were second in the table, behind Notts County, and a 2–1 win at home to Barnsley meant that we were through to the fifth round of the League Cup.

NOVEMBER

A Paul Goddard goal against Bristol Rovers on the first day of the month lifted us to the top of the table, and we were in a relaxed mood two days later when we flew to Romania. The club organized no official travel arrangements for supporters. A small group of fans joined us on the team's charter plane, and their behaviour in Romania was exemplary.

There was little to cheer us in Timisoara, though, when we arrived. It was dusk, and as we drove from the airport we watched dozens of peasant women walking from the fields to their homes miles away.

Our hotel was dimly lit and functional, but the people were hospitable. At the stadium, as we prepared for the kick-off, the 25,000 crowd sang their club song, 'Poli, Poli', to the tune of the Beatles' 'Yellow Submarine'. I felt some sympathy for the people, but they obviously had great strength of character, and that was reflected in the way their team played that day. They had little realistic chance of overhauling a 4–0 deficit. We kept possession and again used Cross's determination and power in the air, but the Romanians fought us to a standstill. We lost 1–0, but it wasn't sufficient to prevent us progressing to the quarter-finals, which would not take place until March.

We returned from Romania and immediately beat Grimsby 2–1 at Upton Park, with Cross scoring twice. Three days later we beat Bristol City 5–0 at Upton Park. This time Goddard scored twice, and Cross, Brooking and Martin got the other goals. Goddard was beginning to look a really superb player. He had been used to Tommy Docherty's style of football at Queen's Park Rangers, and in many ways that was similar to the way we played. Subsequently, he had settled in very quickly. He kept our attack fluent, and the unselfish way he worked for the ball and created chances for others made him a very popular figure, both with the crowd and his teammates. We were on top of Division Two, through to the quarter-finals of both the Cup Winners' Cup and League Cup, and I was beginning to think that it was all going too well for us. Something had to go wrong. It did, against Luton in mid November. We lost 3–2 at Kenilworth Road. Although we then beat Swansea 2–0, we lost the next match 2–0 at Derby and then drew 2–2 at Wrexham. Somehow, though, we still clung to top spot, just above Chelsea.

DECEMBER

The Christmas month started with a real cracker – West Ham v. Tottenham in the League Cup. It was Tottenham's first visit to Upton Park for four years and the ninety-eighth meeting of the two clubs. Some of those matches have been legendary, some merely classics. This one was a classic. At the time, Keith Burkinshaw's Spurs were one of the most attractive sides in the First Division, with players like Ossie Ardiles, Ricardo Villa, Glenn Hoddle and Steve Archibald. They had demolished three of our London neighbours to reach the quarter-finals of the League Cup – Orient, Crystal Palace and Arsenal – and the smart money suggested that we would go the same way. A 36,000 crowd squeezed into Upton Park, with thousands locked out and thousands more watching the closed-circuit TV coverage of the game at North London cinemas. It was a thrilling and absorbing match, fought at tremendous pace, and was decided in the eighty-first minute, when a long, high shot from Cross caught the Tottenham goalkeeper Barry Daines out of position. It was the only goal of the game and it was enough to take us into the League Cup semifinals.

That result restored confidence after our indifferent run of League matches, and four days later we beat Sheffield Wednesday 2–1 at Upton Park. Just before Christmas we drew 0–0 at Blackburn, an important point for us because they were on the fringe of the promotion race. It was a battling performance, typified by the running of Cross and Goddard. Ten minutes from the end, we were holding on to a goalless draw but Blackburn were beginning to break down our defence. Goddard looked exhausted, and I remember watching Cross run from outside right to outside left to chase a full back who was moving forward with the ball.

'Tell Goddard to do his share of the running!' I shouted to him.

When he next had the opportunity, Dave ran across to where I was sitting in the dug-out.

'He's only a youngster and he's knackered,' he said. 'I know what to do. Let him stay up there and I'll do the running.'

David Cross's attitude that day told me a lot about him as a man but also confirmed the depth of spirit and comradeship now resident within that team. I was beginning to think that, this season, we might sustain a promotion challenge until the very end, and when we beat Derby County 3–1 at Upton Park on 20 December we opened up a five-point lead over Chelsea at the top of the Second Division. The win over Derby was our eleventh consecutive home League win of the season – a new club record.

Any sense of euphoria was swiftly dispelled by the next result – a 3–0 defeat against Queen's Park Rangers at Loftus Road on Boxing Day. It was our worst performance of the season. Our cause wasn't helped when we lost Cross with an injury after just fifteen minutes. Even so, Rangers destroyed us with goals from Barry Silkman, Tony Currie and Simon Stainrod. I was bitterly disappointed, not just with the result, but with the performance as well. I kept the players in the dressing room for nearly an hour afterwards.

I didn't always do that. Sometimes, after a defeat, I'd hardly say a word. I'd tell the players that we would sort it out at the training ground on the following Monday. It gave them the weekend to think about the defeat and ponder over their responsibilities. On the Monday I'd say: 'Well, what have you thought about over the weekend?' They knew that I expected some constructive answers.

But that day against Rangers the whole team played poorly, not just one or two individuals. In those circumstances I would hit everyone of them with some relevant points. There are two ways to handle those situations. The first is the subtle approach, which puts the onus on the players to think about the reasons for their defeat. The second is to say immediately after the match: 'There's no way I'm going to stand for that again. Now these are the rules . . .'

Occasionally, of course, I'd take a player to one side on the training pitch. If I felt he was playing under a little pressure I'd say: 'Tell me what's wrong.'

Other players have a tendency to blame everyone else for a defeat. The day comes, though, when I would pick him out in front of all the others in the dressing room to make him aware, very publicly, of his share of the blame.

Those types of assessments after a defeat can make or break a manager. If you go into the dressing room after every defeat with the same routine – 'Now shut up, you lot, and listen' – you're eventually going to have problems. After three or four outbursts like that the players will be sitting there, waiting for you to arrive, saying to themselves: 'The first thing he'll say is "Now shut up, you lot . . ."'

You have to be more subtle than that. You have to make them think. You can't always criticize. You have to stimulate them, too. We were lamentable that day against Rangers, but I knew we were the best team in the Second Division. I stressed that our priority was to win promotion to Division One. At that point we were still involved in four major competitions and, with so many games ahead of us, there was a danger of falling at all four hurdles. I wanted them to be sure in their own minds that nothing mattered quite as much as promotion. I told them that they were a good enough team not to be beaten again in the Second Division that season. That, in fact, was the target I set that Boxing Day – to remain undefeated in the League for the rest of the season. I think the message got home. The following day we beat Orient 2–1 at Upton Park with goals from Paul Allen and Patsy Holland.

JANUARY

Our recent successes on the field had obviously enhanced the club's financial position considerably, and early in the New Year we announced a £500,000 plan to redevelop the West Enclosure terracing under the main stand. It had a capacity of 7,000, but after Jack Petchey, Brian Blower and I had looked at several stadia in the United States during the summer, the club decided to upgrade that area of the ground and install 3,000 seats. I have always been interested in the comfort and safety of spectators and had been impressed by the American facilities. That winter of 1981 was particularly harsh, and often, on a cold January night, my thoughts would go out to the lads on the terraces, stamping their feet and blowing into frozen hands.

The weather that winter threw our fixture schedule into chaos after we failed to beat our Second Division rivals Wrexham in the third round of the FA Cup at Upton Park. Ray Stewart had scored with a penalty in the fifty-ninth minute, but Gareth Davies equalized three minutes before the end. We travelled to Wrexham for the replay three days later and drew 0–0 after extra time. I spun the coin for the choice of venue and the Wrexham manager, Arfon Griffiths, called correctly. So a second replay had to be staged at the Racecourse Ground. We were, of course, the FA Cup holders, and that gives you more reason than most for wanting to do well again in the competition. We didn't want to lose it, but Wrexham were a thorn we couldn't get rid of.

The second replay was twice postponed because of the weather. The first time, we travelled all the way to Wrexham by coach, a tiring journey for the players. As soon as we arrived at our hotel, Wrexham asked me to go to the ground for a pitch inspection. The referee took one look at the pitch and called it off.

We drove straight back to London, having arranged to try again forty-eight hours later. The players passed the time playing cards or Trivial Pursuits, but they were bored with the coach trips. Two days later I wanted a clear indication of the prospects of play before departing from Upton Park. A local Wrexham referee inspected the pitch early in the morning. 'It's waterlogged,' I was told. We didn't travel. Eventually we met in the second replay – sixteen days after the first game – and once again the tie was deadlocked. Then, fourteen minutes into extra time, that old campaigner Dixie McNeil scored and, sadly, we relinquished our hold on the FA Cup. It was a depressing trip home from Wrexham. I don't like to lose in any competition but, looking back, had we progressed in the FA Cup, too, we might have been swamped by the number of games we had to play. In those circumstances you seek some consolation and at that time it was a consoling thought.

Because of our involvement with Wrexham, we played only three League games in January, beating Swansea and Preston comfortably and drawing 1–1 with Notts County at Meadow Lane. The Notts County result was particularly satisfying, because they were third in the table, but in taking a point from them we lost Patsy Holland with a knee injury. Something of an unsung hero, he was none the less one of our most reliable players and was a regular in the team until he collided with the County goalkeeper Raddy Avramovic as he scored our goal. It was a typical piece of cheek, improvisation and bravery by Patsy. He hobbled off the field with a knee injury after fifty-four minutes and, although we didn't know it at the time, he would never play League football again.

Patsy's injury – he was the only player to suffer a serious injury during the season – meant that I had to bring the former Tottenham and Norwich winger Jimmy Neighbour into the team. Jim was a good player, a superb crosser of the ball, but he lacked a little confidence in his own ability. I decided to keep him on the substitute's bench for the first leg of the League Cup semifinal against Coventry at Highfield Road, and brought in Paul Allen, who had recovered from a thigh operation but had made only rare first-team appearances since the FA Cup Final. We took a 2–0 lead against Coventry, through Billy Bonds and a Garry Thompson own goal, but they stormed back at us after the interval, Thompson scoring two more – this time at the right end – and Gerry Daly getting the other goal. Having led 2–0, it was disappointing to return to London facing a 3–2 deficit in the second leg.

FEBRUARY

I played Jimmy Neighbour in the next two Second Division matches, but on the Monday before our second leg against Coventry he came to see me in my office and was obviously a very concerned young man. He was tearful and told me that he didn't think I should select him to face Coventry. He felt he wasn't playing well enough and he didn't want to let the team down. I admired him for being honest with me. I listened sympathetically to what he had to say and offered him a few words of encouragement. I told him to go away and train as normal and let me think about it. Two days later I pinned the team to play Coventry on the noticeboard at Chadwell Heath. His name was on it. This time Allen was substitute.

In the dressing room before the match, Mr Len made a presentation to Billy Bonds who was about to make his 600th first-team appearance for the club. As usual, Bill was an inspiring captain that night before a 36,000 crowd at Upton Park.

In the sixtieth minute of an enthralling match, Goddard scored to draw us level on aggregate at 3–3. With just sixty seconds remaining, and extra time looking a real prospect, the most unlikely match-winner emerged to clinch a place at Wembley – Jimmy Neighbour. He didn't score many goals for West Ham, and none were as important as that one. He was the hero of the evening, and I could have cried for him. After the FA Cup Final and the Charity Shield we were on our way back to Wembley for the third time in the space of ten months.

The confidence of the team didn't need any further boost-

ing but, if it did, it came with that result against Coventry.
We charged through the month of February, beating Shrewsbury 2–0, Chelsea 4–0, Cambridge 4–2 and Watford 2–1.
The team was settled, Neighbour had discovered a little zest
and self-belief, and at the end of the month we had an eight-
point lead over Notts County at the top of Division Two.
There was also a little bonus. The youngsters had reached
the semifinals of the FA Youth Cup. The whole place was
buzzing.

MARCH

I had always valued sound information about opposing teams
we were soon to play, and I learned in March just how costly
it can be to play against unknown opponents. The European
programme had re-opened, and our quarter-final tie was
against the exceptionally talented Dynamo Tbilisi team from
Soviet Georgia. The problem was that the Russian domestic
season had only just resumed after their winter break, but we
tried as hard as we could to get to see them play. They
arranged, at short notice, a couple of friendly matches, but
there was no way that either Eddie Baily or I could get to the
games in time because of the distances involved.

I had to settle for some film clips of their 4–2 defeat of
Liverpool in the European Cup the previous season and their
5–0 win over Waterford of the Republic of Ireland in the Cup
Winners' Cup a few months earlier. It had to do in the
circumstances. Their manager, Nodar Achalkatsi, on the other
hand, had enjoyed the advantage of watching us beat Cambridge 4–2 at Upton Park the month before. For a coach it

makes a big difference to watch the opposition in the flesh playing in a competitive match. I knew, of course, that Tbilisi had a glowing reputation for the quality of their football, and it was easy to see why after just a few minutes of our game at Upton Park. Technically they were a wonderful side, so comfortable and composed on the ball, so full of running off the ball. Their movement off the ball was breathtakingly simple, and it was their angled running across the pitch that made them so difficult to mark. It was an education to watch them, and I was totally stimulated by the skills of players like Aleksandr Chivadze, Vitali Daraselia, David Kipiani and Ramaz Shengalia. They remain one of the finest European sides I've ever seen, and it was a shame when Kipiani's career was ended by a broken leg and a tragedy when Daraselia was killed in a car crash.

The Soviet side led 2–0 after thirty-two minutes, through Chivadze and Vladimir Gutsaev, and although David Cross scored in the fifty-fourth minute, Shengalia scored twice to leave us with a 4–1 deficit to overhaul in the away leg. At the end of the match our crowd of 35,000 gave the Russians a standing ovation. They obviously realized the task we faced, but they also wanted to acknowledge a team of the highest quality. I felt the same; had I been on the terraces I would have applauded them off the field. As it was, I went into the dressing room and told the players they had just been beaten by one of the best teams they would ever play against.

Thankfully, the manner of that defeat didn't affect our League form. Three days later we beat Newcastle 1–0 at Upton Park – our last game before the League Cup Final against Liverpool at Wembley seven days later. We were about to enter one of the most hectic and highly charged periods of my management at West Ham.

We prepared with our usual thoroughness for the Liverpool match. I didn't have to impress on players like Bonds, Brooking or Cross what they faced. They knew precisely what it meant to play Liverpool. With players like Ray Clemence, Kenny Dalglish, Graeme Souness, Alan Hansen, Ray Kennedy and Terry McDermott, they were the best equipped team in the First Division. Then, as now, they were difficult to play against and almost impossible to break down. I decided that we would try to play possession football against players who are the masters of the art. We used our passing qualities to try to contain them and keep the ball away from them. It worked to a degree, and I felt we played well on the day. It was a close match, scoreless after ninety minutes. It was still finely balanced in extra time. Alan Kennedy scored for Liverpool after 117 minutes, and in the last seconds of extra time Ray Stewart, so cool and dependable in difficult circumstances, equalized from the penalty spot. And that was when the fun started. Kennedy's goal should not have been allowed in my opinion. When he struck the ball, his teammate Sammy Lee was crouching on the ground in an offside position in front of our goalkeeper, Phil Parkes. The linesman flagged. The referee, Clive Thomas, moved towards the linesman, signalled that he was overruling him and then pointed to the centre circle. I couldn't believe he had given the goal. In the mayhem on the pitch at the end of the game, Clive came over to me and began to explain his actions.

'Leave it, Clive,' I said. 'If you watch the match on TV tomorrow you'll understand why we feel cheated.' I told him that we felt cheated. I didn't accuse him of cheating. The misunderstanding arose through misinterpretation of remarks made in the heat of the moment, seconds after the match. I was not referring to him as an individual, but to the incident. I was hurt the following morning to read headlines in the Sunday newspapers like 'Big Bad John' and 'Lyall Called Me a Cheat.' Clive had made his comments to the Press after the match as he was entitled to. To give him credit, he also said that the linesman had waved his flag and that Lee was lying on the pitch in an offside position, though, he argued, he was not interfering with play. He also admitted that it was a mistake not to have consulted the linesman when asked to do so by the West Ham players.

The outcome of all this emotion in the moments immediately after a high-octane match was this: I was cautioned for the first time in my career by Clive Thomas and, as a result of that, faced a charge of bringing the game into disrepute. There was also a chance I could be banned from the touchline for the replay at Villa Park. Two days later, as the tabloids had a field-day with the Thomas–Lyall affair, I flew to Russia knowing that I faced a Football Association hearing.

In three games in Europe we had travelled across the width of the continent, from Madrid in the West, through Romania in the centre, to Tbilisi in the east. The trip to Soviet Georgia for the second leg of the quarter-final was, logistically, easily the most formidable. The return journey to Timisoara had taken thirty-five hours. We spent nearly that long simply travelling out to Tbilisi. We hit the most incredible snags that interrupted schedules, frayed tempers and brought physical discomfort. We had to fly via Moscow, where we spent hours negotiating passport control. One stony-faced passport official didn't believe that Bobby Barnes was the same person as the one photographed in his passport. Bobby had just had a crinkly hair cut, and the picture in his passport was of a fresh-faced youth. George Scanlon, our interpreter, assured the official that it was indeed the same person and hustled Bobby through.

The biggest problem, though, was the weather. Moscow was snowbound and the de-icing machine was working furiously to get the ice off the wings of our aircraft. After a three-hour wait, the authorities shut the airport for the night. We were stranded in the transit lounge. Finally, George, who was a senior lecturer in Russian at Liverpool University and had played football for Cambridge and Pegasus, persuaded the airport authorities to allow us to remove some of our own food from the plane. We needed to supply a doctor's certificate for this simple exercise. While the food was being prepared he and I visited an airport hotel, because it was obvious by now that we would have to stay the night. I remember stepping, bleary-eyed, from the airport bus outside the hotel straight into a waist-high snowdrift. It was an austere hotel, but better than spending the night in the transit lounge. We went back to the airport, where we found the players walking one at a time, under the vigilant eyes of the guards, to the toilets. We took the players by bus to the airport hotel, and they got to bed at midnight, London time. We were up six hours later, but had to wait a further six hours before taking off from Moscow. We finally arrived in Tbilisi late in the afternoon, nearly a day late. The weather was warm, and officials from the host club, who had been waiting at the airport all the previous night, extended a welcome that matched the temperature.

It was hardly the best way to prepare for a match but, after our 4–1 home defeat, the players wanted to salvage a little pride. Realistically, we had little chance of securing the result that would take us into the semifinals. So we felt little pressure. We simply wanted to make a point.

We played well, retaining possession, drawing them into us and hoping to catch them on the break. That's just what we did. It wasn't quite the spectacular footballing showpiece we had seen at Upton Park, but none the less I was thrilled when substitute Stuart Pearson, making a rare first-team appearance following a lengthy knee injury, scored the only goal of the game. The match was played in a wonderful spirit, exemplified by the spontaneous exchange of shirts between the players as they were applauded off the field by 80,000 fans in the magnificent Lenin Stadium. The journey home was less traumatic. We flew back through the night, arriving at Stanstead at 7 a.m. A 1–0 win over a team of Tbilisi's quality was adequate consolation.

The players were exhausted, and it showed three days later when we drew 1–1 with Oldham at Upton Park. But Paul Goddard's goal gave us a ten-point lead at the top of the table, and at that point, in the middle of March, we were already guaranteed promotion to Division One. A week later we drew 1–1 at Bolton – our eleventh successive Second Division match without defeat.

APRIL

When we faced Liverpool in the League Cup Final replay at Villa Park on the opening day of the month I had been cleared by the FA to take my usual place on the touchline bench. To give Clive Thomas full credit, at the FA hearing he didn't criticize me and even suggested that he was probably wrong to have walked across to me so soon after the end of the match. He accepted the responsibility and fortunately I was completely exonerated. There was no animosity and no loss of face by either of us. It was a fair hearing, and I took along my youth team manager, Tony Carr, as a witness. After the hearing, he and I had lunch with Clive in a hotel just round the corner from the FA headquarters in Lancaster Gate, and we parted the best of friends.

Before that incident, I had always got along well with Clive. I respected him as a referee and regarded him as one of the best officials in the game. He was a FIFA referee and had officiated at the 1974 and 1978 World Cup Finals. He knew his business – just as I knew mine. Looking back, I still feel the goal should have been disallowed. The single most important question to arise from that incident remains unanswerable. When is an offside player interfering with play? There is no clear answer. It is a matter of opinion. It is a grey area within the laws of the game. But as the late Liverpool manager Bill Shankly once remarked: 'If he's not interfering, what's he doing on the field?'

Clive was the referee again for the replay and handled the game impeccably. We started brilliantly, Goddard scoring with a near-post header from Neighbour's cross. Liverpool, with Ian Rush in their attack this time, simply stepped up a gear. Dalglish equalized after twenty-five minutes with a volleyed goal as good as I've ever seen, and three minutes later Hansen scored a second. We nagged away at them in the second half, but couldn't disrupt their rhythm or disturb their composure. They beat us 2–1, and I had no complaints at the end of the match.

We still had the Second Division Championship to clinch

and we did that in some style. We won all four of our League games in April – Cross scoring those costly four goals in a 5–1 win at Grimsby, and Goddard avenging our Boxing Day defeat by scoring all three against his old club, QPR, at Upton Park. The other results on 11 April, when we won at Grimsby, ensured that we could not be overtaken. We were declared Champions that day.

MAY

The players had two targets remaining – to finish the rest of the season unbeaten and to accumulate a club-record number of points. They did both. They hadn't lost in the Second Division since the Boxing Day defeat against Rangers. In our last three matches they beat Wrexham – a sweet win after our FA Cup exit against them – drew at Cardiff and then beat Sheffield Wednesday. That stretched our run of unbeaten Second Division matches to eighteen. We finished the season with sixty-six points (in the days of two points for a win), beating the previous club record of fifty-seven points. In all we played sixty matches that season. It was exhausting, exhilarating and immensely satisfying. At the end of the season, nine journalists, most of whom had travelled with the club across Europe, presented me with an inscribed gold ring. After some of the excesses I had experienced from the Press that season it was a warm and meaningful gesture. I have always felt it important to have a good relationship with the Press, and particularly the local reporters. In my case this meant Trevor Smith, who has been covering West Ham for thirty-four years for the *Ilford Recorder*, Ken Dyer, who at the time wrote for the *Southend Evening Echo*, and Steve Bacon, who supplied the local papers with photographs. They travelled with me on the team coach, and I felt they were particularly important to the club because they informed the local public of West Ham news at all the different levels – not just the big names and the big matches.

I left the newspapermen, the telephone and all the other little problems behind and decided to take a holiday with Yvonne. I was delighted when the youngsters beat Spurs 2–1 on aggregate in the FA Youth Cup Final. I was further delighted when Alvin Martin made his debut for England against Brazil at Wembley. It had been a dream season. My only sadness was Patsy Holland's injury.

JUNE

Fishing. The best result of the season – a double-figure carp.

THE CHAMPIONSHIP SEASON, 1980–81:
COMPLETE RESULTS

─── SECOND DIVISION ───

H	Luton	L	1–2	Stewart
A	Bristol City	D	1–1	Cross
A	Preston	D	0–0	
H	Notts County	W	4–0	Goddard 2, Cross, Stewart
A	Chelsea	W	1–0	own goal
H	Shrewsbury	W	3–0	Cross, Goddard, own goal
H	Watford	W	3–2	Barnes, Brooking, Cross
A	Cambridge	W	2–1	Cross, Goddard
A	Newcastle	D	0–0	
H	Cardiff	W	1–0	Neighbour
H	Blackburn	W	2–0	Cross 2
A	Oldham	D	0–0	
H	Bolton	W	2–1	Pike, own goal
A	Bristol Rvrs	W	1–0	Goddard
H	Grimsby	W	2–1	Cross 2
H	Bristol City	W	5–0	Goddard 2, Brooking, Martin, Cross
A	Luton	L	2–3	Brooking 2
H	Swansea	W	2–0	Cross, Goddard
A	Derby	L	0–2	
A	Wrexham	D	2–2	Devonshire, Goddard
H	Sheff. Wed.	W	2–1	Brooking, Holland
A	Blackburn	D	0–0	
H	Derby	W	3–1	Brooking, Cross, Goddard
A	QPR	L	0–3	
H	Orient	W	2–1	Allen, Holland
A	Swansea	W	3–1	Brooking, Cross, Pike
A	Notts County	D	1–1	Holland
H	Preston	W	5–0	Devonshire 2, Pike, Goddard, Lampard
A	Shrewsbury	W	2–0	Cross, Devonshire
H	Chelsea	W	4–0	Brooking 2, Cross, Devonshire
H	Cambridge	W	4–2	Stewart 2, Devonshire, Goddard
A	Watford	W	2–1	Cross 2
H	Newcastle	W	1–0	Cross
H	Oldham	D	1–1	Goddard

THE CHAMPIONSHIP SEASON

A	Bolton	D	1–1	Brooking
H	Bristol Rvrs	W	2–0	Goddard, Pike
A	Grimsby	W	5–1	Cross 4, Pike
A	Orient	W	2–0	Neighbour, Pike
H	QPR	W	3–0	Goddard 3
H	Wrexham	W	1–0	Stewart
A	Cardiff	D	0–0	
A	Sheff. Wed.	W	1–0	Morgan

FA CUP

Round three	H	Wrexham	D	1–1	Stewart
Replay	A	Wrexham	D	0–0	
Replay	A	Wrexham	L	0–1	

LEAGUE CUP

Round two	A	Burnley	W	2–0	Goddard, Cross
Round two	H	Burnley	W	4–0	Stewart, Goddard, Pike, own goal
Round three	A	Charlton	W	2–1	Cross 2
Round four	H	Barnsley	W	2–1	Martin, Cross
Round five	H	Tottenham	W	1–0	Cross
Semifinal	A	Coventry	L	2–3	Bonds, own goal
Semifinal	H	Coventry	W	2–0	Goddard, Neighbour
Final	Wembley	Liverpool	D	1–1	Stewart
Replay	Villa Park	Liverpool	L	1–2	Goddard

EUROPEAN CUP WINNERS' CUP

Round one	A	Castilla	L	1–3	Cross
	H	Castilla	W	5–1	Cross 3, Pike, Goddard
Round two	H	Timisoara	W	4–0	Bonds, Cross, Goddard, Stewart
	A	Timisoara	L	0–1	
Round three	H	Tbilisi	L	1–4	Cross
	A	Tbilisi	W	1–0	Pearson

THE **BIG** OFFER

It was June 1984. I was pottering about in the garden, when Yvonne called out from the house and told me I was wanted on the telephone. As a football manager there are times when you curse the telephone. It can be an intrusion on the few spare hours you get. On the other hand, it is an essential tool of the trade. To be honest, though, the occasions when my mind was completely free of the job were few. That day, as I repaired some fencing, I was pondering over the new season. We had consolidated our First Division status comfortably enough, finishing ninth, eighth and ninth in our opening three seasons among the élite of the game. But there is a big difference between that and sustaining a realistic challenge for the Championship against teams like Liverpool, Everton, Manchester United and Nottingham Forest. Like all First Division managers, my ambition was to win the Championship.

The man on the telephone that day was Dennis Signy, the journalist and close friend, who years earlier had tipped me off about the availability of Paul Goddard. This time he told me that Queen's Park Rangers, who were looking for a manager to replace Terry Venables, wanted to talk to me. Was I interested? It was a suggestion that took me totally by surprise. I had given no thought to leaving West Ham. There was no reason to. I was happy and, as far as I could ascertain, the board of directors were more than satisfied with my contribution. My contract didn't expire until the following June, but Mr Len and I had already tentatively discussed the situation, quite a normal procedure at Upton Park.

Terry Venables had enjoyed great success with QPR – FA Cup runners-up in 1982 and Second Division champions in 1983 – and had now accepted a fabulous offer to manage Barcelona in Spain. I knew they were looking for a manager, but newspaper speculation insisted that Luton's David Pleat was the number-one contender. Now, suddenly, I was in the frame. I knew Dennis's information had to be correct, because he was very close at the time to the Queen's Park Rangers chairman, Jim Gregory. There was nothing unusual in being approached by another club – all managers receive similar calls during their careers – but I realized immediately that this was a serious attempt by Rangers to offer me the job. I told Dennis that he would have to ask Rangers to make an official approach to the West Ham chairman, Len Cearns, if they wanted to take the matter any further. I was not prepared to discuss anything in a back-door fashion. I made that quite clear to him. He told me he would phone Mr Gregory. A few hours later, my day in the garden was again interrupted by the telephone. This time it was Mr Len, who wanted to see me immediately. I got into the car and drove to his house in Chigwell. He told me that Queen's Park Rangers wanted me as their next manager. He didn't want to lose me, but he was prepared to let me discuss it with them. He told me that he had given Rangers permission to talk to me.

I was grateful to him. I had no real intention of leaving West Ham at the time, but I was flattered that they should approach me and I felt that at least I should have the opportunity to talk to them and see what they had to offer. I then called Jim Gregory, and he asked me to go to his house. I knew him as a very shrewd negotiator from the dealings I had had with him during the transfers of Phil Parkes and Paul Goddard. I didn't know him socially, but his business acumen was one of the things that appealed to me. He had been at Rangers for nearly twenty years and was the longest-serving club chairman in the Football League. He was a progressive thinker and had virtually rebuilt the club from top to bottom. He was a rich and successful businessman, and I was not surprised by the magnificence of his house in Wimbledon when I finally pulled on to the driveway.

We sat in his lounge and he came straight to the point.

'I want you to be my next manager,' he said. 'This is what I'm offering you . . .'

It was a quite extraordinary offer, practically doubling the money I was earning at West Ham. Over the five years of the proposed contract I would have been £200,000 better off. It would have put me among the First Division's mega-earners, like Brian Clough at Nottingham Forest and Ron Atkinson at Manchester United. I could have worked the five years of the contract and then, had I wanted to, retired in the summer of 1989, instead of suddenly finding myself discarded by West Ham.

I just listened to him. I didn't really have to negotiate. When he finished outlining the financial details I asked about a car.

'Oh! Sorry. The car, of course,' he said. 'There's a new Jaguar. You can have it by the end of the week.'

It was an impressive offer. He asked me about a house. I told him that I enjoyed keeping fish and said that, if I accepted, I would probably look for a house on the west side of London with a small lake. He called his son into the room.

'See if you can find John a house with a lake,' he told him.

I couldn't argue with anything about the personal details. I just nodded my agreement as he went through them. But I wanted to know what he thought about the game, his own team and the future of the club. With Terry Venables as manager, the club had enjoyed great success, he told me. He wanted to build on that. One of the things that had always impressed me about QPR was the way they had struck a sensible balance between financing ground and team improvements. They had spent enormous sums of money upgrading the Loftus Road stadium, but that investment had in no way damaged the team. They had spent big money on top-class players – £400,000 for Tony Currie from Leeds is an example – but they had capitalized on the sales potential of players, too. The best example of that was the £1.25 million they received from Arsenal for Clive Allen. Jim Gregory had rebuilt the stadium, rebuilt the team and, at the same time, maintained a level of success on the field. I felt the club had exciting possibilities.

He made it clear to me that money would be available to buy the best players. He wanted to challenge the élite clubs in London, Liverpool and Manchester. It was a manager's dream. The only problem for me was going to be making a decision. I told him I would think about it. I left his house in Wimbledon with a smile on my face.

He had told me that I could appoint my own coaching staff, and as I drove home to share the news with Yvonne, I began addressing this problem. I had four key men on my staff at West Ham – the three coaches, Ronnie Boyce, Mick McGiven and Tony Carr, and my chief scout, Eddie Baily. They had all provided me with invaluable support over the years, but I knew that if I accepted the QPR offer I would not be able to take all four. I thought about it and made up my mind to ask Eddie Baily and Mick McGiven to join me. Ronnie and Tony were no less able, but I felt that, as former West Ham players, they would maintain the traditional continuity at the club if they stayed.

Later that day, Yvonne and I discussed the Rangers offer at great length. She knew I was in a dilemma. I can remember thinking at one stage that I wished the offer had not been made. Then there would have been no decision to make. But, for us both, it was the pot of gold at the end of the rainbow. I had been working long hours since the age of 24 and had realized years ago that Yvonne and Murray had both had to make sacrifices because of my job. They had missed a great deal in the way of family life so that I could pursue my career. I felt this offer would help make amends to some degree. Apart from anything else, it provided the family with long-term security and meant that I might be able to retire earlier than I had intended. That would give Yvonne and me time together. I think I had reached a stage where I needed to look beyond my own feelings and put my family first. There had been many years when I had not put them first.

West Ham had treated me wonderfully, but, as much as I loved the club and everything about it, I knew I had to be realistic. The QPR offer had been made in a correct and official manner. Financially, the terms offered to me were superb. The club had enormous potential, on and off the field, and I felt my family would benefit in the long term if I accepted. I called Jim Gregory and told him I would like to accept his offer of a job.

Then I went to see Mr Len and told him I wanted to go to Rangers. Would the club release me from my contract? He said he would have to call a board meeting. A few days later he told me that the board had met and decided that they wanted me to stay at Upton Park and honour the remaining year of my contract. I was disappointed and upset. I had hoped they would agree to release me. Mr Len said that if I insisted on joining Rangers, West Ham would demand £150,000 compensation.

'I have to think of my family,' I told him.

'I have to think of the club,' he replied. 'If you go, there are certain conditions that QPR will have to meet.'

I was already beginning to feel uncomfortable about the situation. I went back to Jim Gregory and told him of West Ham's reaction to my request. He then spoke to Mr Len about compensation, but I sensed that it would be wrong for me, and both clubs, if I became a commodity in an auction. I didn't want that. I didn't want to provoke a situation where two clubs were fighting over my services. I didn't want to be responsible for a major row between the two clubs. The situation was becoming increasingly complicated. There was even a threat that I could be the subject of a Football Association investigation into an alleged illegal approach. Eventually I called Jim Gregory.

'Forget it, Jim,' I said. 'I'm sorry, but I don't want anyone bartering over me. I'm going to stay at West Ham.'

It was no hardship to turn down the offer. Had circumstances been different I would have accepted it, because of the generosity of the offer and the benefits that would have brought to my family. But I had a marvellous job at West Ham. I had been there twenty-nine years and was the Football League's second longest-serving manager, behind Southampton's Lawrie McMenemy. I had made my decision and, as far as I was concerned, that was the end of the matter. I was going to devote all my energies to West Ham.

Jim Gregory was disappointed, but he's not the sort of man who wastes time on self-pity. A few weeks later he appointed the former Tottenham and England captain Alan Mullery, just dismissed at Crystal Palace, as manager. Alan was given a one-year contract, but in December, after a difficult first half to the season, he left the club and coach Frank Sibley was put in temporary control.

So, once again, Rangers were looking for a manager. Don Revie, the former England manager, was linked with the job, and as my contract with West Ham now had only six months to run the newspapers were again speculating about the prospects of me going to Loftus Road after all. But, because of the gentleman's agreement between club chairmen not to poach each other's managers during the course of the season, I was off-limits to QPR. At the time I didn't appreciate all the fresh speculation. I had been twenty-four hours away from joining Rangers in the summer, when the West Ham board vetoed the move. For me, and West Ham, it served no purpose to raise all that again, especially as I was now negotiating a new contract with Mr Len. My feeling at the time was that I would now probably stay at West Ham for the remainder of my working life.

During the summer, after Keith Burkinshaw had left Tottenham, I had also been linked in the newspapers with the job that eventually went to Peter Shreeves. I never encouraged speculation of this kind and always wanted to conduct my personal affairs privately. But now, of course, my contractual negotiations with West Ham were a matter of some public interest. I had asked Mr Len for a five-year contract but, when he came to me with the club's offer, it was for only three years. I didn't sign it immediately. I wanted a little more security than that. The talks with Mr Len continued through most of that winter. They were the most protracted contract negotiations I went through during my years at West Ham. I think I always intended to sign, but I wanted the terms to be right.

Another concern for me was our form in the First Division. We were playing badly at the time, and between November and March in a winter programme severely disrupted by the weather, we won just two of sixteen games. One day Billy Bonds came to see me in my little office at Chadwell Heath.

'John, are you going to sign?' he asked. 'The lads are constantly discussing it in the dressing room and I think it's affecting the way they play. They feel unsettled and unsure.'

I listened carefully to what he had to say. I trusted Bill. He was a good captain and, if he said that, I realized there had to be some deep feeling about the issue among the players.

'Tell them not to worry, Bill, I'll sign it,' I told him.

I would probably have signed anyway, but Bill's intervention made me realize that I owed something to the players. 'They've kept me employed here for five years,' I thought.

A few days later, Mr Len and I reached a compromise, and I signed a new four-year contract in March 1985. It was due to expire in June 1989.

Fortunately, the team's form showed signs of revival. We beat Wimbledon 5–1 in an FA Cup fifth-round replay at Upton Park, Alan Devonshire making only his second appearance of the season, but lost 4–2 to Manchester United at Old Trafford in the sixth round, when Norman Whiteside scored a hat-trick. Our League form improved – we lost just six of our last fourteen games – and we finished sixteenth, safe from relegation but clearly not good enough.

One of the problems we faced that season was overcoming the loss of two of our most experienced and creative midfield players. In January of the previous season Alan Devonshire had suffered an appalling knee injury in an FA Cup third-round tie against Wigan at Upton Park. He had spent months in hospital and at rehabilitation centres. He was a stoical lad, but he loathed lying in a hospital bed.

I remember getting a call from him one morning shortly after he'd had a serious knee operation.

'John, get up here quick,' he said. 'The knee's gone again.' I was puzzled. I couldn't understand how his knee could suffer any further damage while he was lying motionless in hospital.

I went to the hospital where I found him lying in bed, leg encased in plaster, feeling sorry for himself. As I arrived a young nurse walked past his bed.

'John! John! That's the one!' he hissed. 'She banged my leg. Keep her away from me. John, you've got to get me moved or I'll never play again!'

He was still heavily sedated from the previous day's operation and wasn't fully aware of what he was saying. I talked to him and calmed him down. When I left, the ward sister pulled me to one side and laughed.

'Are you the manager of West Ham?' she asked. 'How you put up with him I don't know.'

He wasn't a good patient, and although he couldn't remember the incident, he later returned to the hospital with flowers for the staff. It was a typical gesture by Alan. The fact was, he received excellent treatment. They nursed him back to health and, of course, he went on to play another 100 games for West Ham.

What none of us knew at the time, though, was that his injury would hasten the retirement of Trevor Brooking. After a nineteen-year playing career, Trevor retired in May 1984, at the age of 35. He was in a quandary. He felt West Ham were close to having a team capable of challenging for the title, and he wanted to be part of it. But he knew that he had, perhaps, only one season of top-class football left in his legs. He felt Devonshire was a critical member of the team and, had it not been for the injury Alan received against Wigan, Trevor would have stayed with West Ham for another year. But he feared, and he was right, that Alan's injury would keep him out of action for more than a year. So he decided to announce his retirement. That meant, of course, that we were without our two most creative attacking players throughout the season 1984–5. I risked Devonshire in two FA Cup matches against Wimbledon, but it was probably a little too early to bring him back, and it wasn't until the start of the following season that he was fit enough to play regularly.

I was glad to get 1984–5 behind me. Like most people, I like to feel settled and secure, and it had been an unsettling time. One of West Ham's great strengths as a club is its stability. I felt as if I was part of the fabric of the club and, if the QPR bid had tugged at a few strands, it was now behind me. It was the only occasion as a manager that I had seriously considered leaving. As a young player of 20, Brighton had looked at me in the West Ham reserve team and asked Ron Greenwood if he would sell me. Jackie Burkett was in the first team and restricting my chances, and Ron had promised that he would tell me if any other clubs showed an interest. He told me when the Brighton manager George Curtis made an enquiry.

'You are at a good club, in a First Division set-up, and I think you should stay,' Ron advised me. But he told me to discuss it with my father and think about the offer for twenty-four hours. I went home and spoke to my dad. He rarely got involved in any discussion about my future, simply because he didn't feel qualified. On this occasion, however, he ventured an opinion.

'West Ham were especially considerate when you had your knee operation. Are you sure you will be moving to something better?' The next day I went back to see Ron and told him I wanted to stay.

Years later, when Frank O'Farrell, a former teammate at Upton Park, was manager of Manchester United, he considered offering me a coaching job at Old Trafford. I was Ron's assistant at the time, and I remember travelling with him on a train to the Midlands when he asked me if I would be interested in going to Manchester United. This, of course, was in the days of Bobby Charlton, George Best and Denis Law, and United were just about the most glamorous club in world football. Frank needed a coach and, when asked, Ron had recommended me.

'It's a marvellous opportunity for you,' he said. I looked out of the window as the train pulled through the countryside. It took me five minutes to make up my mind.

'I'll stay,' I said.

That opportunity – the Rangers bid – and one half-hearted enquiry from Glasgow Rangers – made by a newspaperman when John Greig left Ibrox – were the only times I ever stirred myself sufficiently to think of leaving West Ham. There were the back-door approaches that all managers and coaches receive, but my policy was to dismiss them out of hand.

Over the years I had learned to value all that West Ham stood for, and my ambition, as we went into the season 1985–6, burned as brightly as ever. I wanted to win the League Championship for West Ham. If we had lost Brooking and Devonshire the previous season, there had been some consolation. Paul Allen, who had been in and out of the side since he was 17, had finally established himself as a first-team regular. There had been similar progress, too, for Alan Dickens, an intelligent, upright, graceful midfield player in the Brooking mould. Finally, young Tony Cottee, short and powerfully built, had adapted quickly to the demands of First Division football and was drawing comparisons with the great West German striker Gerd Muller.

He scored twenty-four goals in first-team games in the season 1984–5, and Paul Goddard scored fourteen. Ray Stewart had scored seven penalties but, those three players apart, our goalscoring returns from the other players were poor. The absence of Brooking and Devonshire may have been a significant factor, but I knew that to have a realistic chance of the First Division title I would have to sign another player with a goalscoring pedigree.

I needed a player who could operate just behind the front two of Goddard and Cottee, and score goals, too. The player

I wanted was Frank McAvennie. Our Scottish scouts had been tracking him for a long time. Several other clubs were interested, notably Luton Town. I had watched him myself and knew that he could play either as a striker or as a midfield player attacking from deep positions. I called my pal Jim McLean, the manager of Dundee United, and described the type of player I was searching for.

'The best in that category is McAvennie at St Mirren,' he said without hesitation. I spoke to another friend, Alex Ferguson, then manager of Aberdeen, and he confirmed all that Jim had told me. The two Scottish managers agreed that McAvennie had charisma. The crowds loved him and there was always a buzz when he had the ball at his feet.

I called the St Mirren manager, Alex Miller. He was resigned to losing McAvennie, and we agreed a fee of £340,000. There was a problem, though. That day, McAvennie had travelled south for talks with Luton. There was little I could do but wait for the outcome of those negotiations. That evening I sat at home waiting for the telephone to ring. At 10 o'clock Alex Miller called to say they were still talking. An hour later he called again to report there had been no change in the situation. Then, just after midnight, he told me: 'Frank's decided he's not going to sign. Do you still want to talk to him?'

'Yes, of course,' I replied.

'When?' Alex asked.

'Now,' I said, and we arranged to meet at the Toddington service restaurant on the M1 motorway an hour later. I got into the car, drove to Toddington and went into the cafeteria. The place was practically deserted at that time of the morning, apart from a waitress, a lorry driver and two policemen. I sat quietly in a corner until four gentlemen dressed in suits arrived by mini cab. They were Alex Miller, a St Mirren director, Frank and his adviser, Bill McMurdo. I joined them and we talked over cups of tea. By 4 a.m. it was all agreed. What impressed me about Frank was his sense of independence. He obviously had an excellent relationship with his adviser, but he stressed continually that the final decision would be his and his alone. It was light as I drove home past Woburn Abbey. The deer were playing in the park. I felt quite pleased with myself.

Frank and his entourage flew back to Glasgow early that morning, and I arranged to meet Alex at the Excelsior Hotel opposite the airport later in the afternoon to complete the formalities. When I arrived at the hotel, Frank and Alex were waiting for me. The signing of the forms took no more than a few minutes. We all shook hands and I walked back into the airport and boarded the shuttle to London that I'd flown up on. As I ducked through the aircraft door, the stewardess looked at me with a puzzled smile.

'Didn't you just come up on this plane?' she asked.

The following day Frank flew down to London and I picked him up at the airport. We drove back through the centre of London, because he wanted to look at the King's Road. I was to learn that he was a fashion-conscious lad, very concerned about his appearance. I could tell that he was thrilled to be in London. We drove through the City, where the traffic was particularly heavy. Passing us on the opposite side of the road was a convoy of black limousines with police motorcycle escort. Sitting in the back of one of the cars was Princess Diana. She passed within a few feet of us. Frank was impressed.

'This is London, Frank,' I said.

He signed for us in June 1985 and looked bright, sharp and enthusiastic in pre-season training. A month later I was disappointed to lose Paul Allen, who had just re-established himself in the first team after missing half a season through injury. He wanted to move, and the fact that Tottenham and Liverpool were interested increased his desire to get away from Upton Park. He eventually signed for Spurs, who were told by the transfer tribunal to pay £400,000 plus an extra £50,000 if he played ten times for England.

I compensated for that loss by investing half the money we received in Mark Ward, who was then a little-known winger at Oldham Athletic. Our scouts in the north had been watching him since he was a youth, first with Everton and later with non-League Northwich Victoria. Eddie Baily had watched him in the last three games of the previous season and had been so impressed with his speed and tenacity that he recommended we sign him. Looking back, there were a few raised eyebrows when we paid £220,000.

So, when we finally faced Birmingham City at St Andrews, in our opening First Division match of 1985–6, it was with a completely reshaped attacking formation. Ward played wide on the right, and Devonshire, now completely recovered from his terrible injury, was wide on the left. Goddard and Cottee were the two central strikers, with McAvennie providing support just behind them. It had looked a promising formation in pre-season friendly matches, but looks can be deceptive. We lost 1–0 to Birmingham, who had been promoted from Division Two the previous season. Worse still, Goddard dislocated his shoulder in that match and didn't play again that season, apart from a handful of appearances as substitute.

I returned gloomily to London from Birmingham that Saturday evening. I realized that I had little option other than to change the formation and play McAvennie as a striker alongside Cottee in our home match against QPR three days later. That's what I did. McAvennie scored twice and we won 3–1. The only disappointment was the crowd – just 15,500 for our first home game of the season. By the end of the season the figure would be double.

We lost our next two games, at home to Luton and away to Manchester United and by the time we drew 2–2 against Liverpool at Upton Park we were seventeenth in the table. But there was a consolation – Frank scored twice against the champions, who had two of the best centre backs in the business in Mark Lawrenson and Alan Hansen.

After five games Cottee hadn't scored and, despite his youth and exuberance, he looked under pressure. I took him out of the starting line-up for the next match against Southampton, made him substitute, and brought in the reserve striker Greg Campbell. Greg played for an hour and then went down with cramp. I sent Cottee on and he looked much sharper. Frank scored again in a 1–1 draw. He would have had a hat-trick but for the agility of Peter Shilton in the Southampton goal.

The decision to relegate Tony to the substitute's bench had the desired effect. He was brilliant in the next game, when he and Frank scored a goal each in a 2–2 draw against Sheffield Wednesday at Hillsborough. They were beginning to look an effective partnership; ironic, really, when you consider they were playing together at the front only because of Paul Goddard's injury.

They again scored a goal apiece a week later, in a 3–0

home win over Leicester City. They both had terrific pace and we were learning to exploit it. Rather than play low passes to their feet, a situation which would have involved them in battles against bigger defenders, we were trying to play balls into the spaces between defenders. We had worked at this for weeks in training, with the midfield players running at the defence with the ball before sliding it between the centre back and the full back for Frank or Tony to chase. Alan Devonshire and Mark Ward invariably supplied the service and did the job well.

Tony was sharp enough and strong enough to get behind defenders, and he had a thirst for goals that was quite extraordinary. He catalogued all the goals he scored, both mentally and in a cuttings book at home. Where his goals are concerned he has the brain of a computer. He can recall them all instantly. I used to chide him:

'I thought there was a suspicion of offside about that goal you scored against Spurs.'

'I scored that, no question,' he would reply. Then he would proceed to explain precisely why he wasn't offside and convince you that it was, indeed, a genuine goal.

He was a calculating finisher. Put the ball into a little space in the penalty area and he would deal with it clinically. He had been a sensational goalscorer as a 14-year-old, and when he was scoring he was as happy as a sandboy. In his early days at West Ham I'd been impressed with his ambition and his sense of urgency. He wanted to get on with his career. He didn't play much reserve-team football, because when his opportunity came in the first team he snatched at it and gave me no chance to leave him out. He made his debut against Tottenham at Upton Park on New Year's Day, 1983. He scored – inevitably.

Although he's a natural goalscorer, he's not a natural team player. Some strikers create many of their own goals, but Tony is largely reliant on a good service. He's an intelligent lad with an open mind, and I tried to introduce other dimensions to his game.

Like all goalscorers he suffered barren patches, and I used to stress to him that, in the lean times, the team player can at least draw some satisfaction from his all-round contribution, even if he hasn't scored. He was trying to broaden his game when we sold him to Everton for £2 million. I was particularly encouraged when we won 2–1 at Oxford. He scored one of the goals, but spent the last quarter of the game filling in admirably at left back. He wanted to be more than just a goalscorer. He wanted to receive the ball well, be comfortable with it and create chances for others. I'm convinced that in time his all-round game will be as effective as his goalscoring.

By the time we played that game at Oxford in November we had climbed to fifth in the table. We had been unbeaten in twelve games, and Tony and Frank were in full flow. Tony had scored nine goals and Frank fourteen in the First Division – and they enjoyed the rivalry.

Tony, of course, was a product of the Upton Park youth scheme, while Frank was the glamorous big-money signing. Suggestions were beginning to creep into the newspapers that their rivalry wasn't so friendly. I have never understood how that came about, because they were good pals, on and off the field. Of course, there are times in a match when one striker will look at the other and say: 'If you'd given the ball to me then I could have scored.' But that situation arises all the time in football. Perhaps the great goalscorers require a little greed in their make-up. But as for them being bitter rivals . . . well,

I thought at the time I read about it in the newspapers that it was quite absurd. I remember Frank mentioning it to me one day.

'Did you see that story in the paper the other day?' he asked. 'Strange story that. The day it appeared Tony and I were playing golf together.'

Although we lost 1–0 to Manchester United at Old Trafford in the third round of the Milk Cup at the end of October, November was a memorable month for us in the First Division. We beat Everton, Oxford, Watford, Coventry and West Bromwich Albion, and moved to third place in the table. The emphatic 4–0 win over Albion was particularly satisfying, because we had to play without McAvennie. Earlier in the month he had scored for Scotland on his international debut in their 2–0 win over Australia at Hampden Park in a World Cup play-off match.

Scotland, quite naturally, wanted to take him with them for the second leg against Australia in Melbourne. I'd never refused a West Ham player permission to play for his country in an important game and, although it meant we would be without him for at least one and possibly two matches, I agreed to his release. Frank was away for ten days and just three days after Scotland's goalless draw in Melbourne ensured their qualification for the 1986 World Cup, we were due to play QPR at Loftus Road. He arrived home, sleepless, at midday on Friday, little more than twenty-four hours before we were due to play Rangers. 'Yes, I want to play,' he insisted. He played and scored in a 1–0 win.

We didn't lose again until we visited White Hart Lane on Boxing Day, when a Steve Perryman goal, his only goal of the season, gave Tottenham a 1–0 win. That defeat ended a run of eighteen unbeaten First Division games, a new record for the West Ham history books. McAvennie and Cottee were dominating the headlines, but what gave me equal pleasure was the form of our defence. The enduring excellence of Phil Parkes, now 35, was a major factor, though the back four of Ray Stewart, Alvin Martin, Tony Gale and Steve Walford had formed a sound and settled unit. Perhaps one of the most significant features of the entire season was the fact that the team remained largely injury-free. Of course, we lost Goddard in the opening game, and at the time I viewed that as a sinister omen. But we suffered no other serious injuries, and the fact that I was able to use the same thirteen players for the vast majority of our games gave us the sort of stability that builds confidence and team spirit and wins matches.

This, I felt, was perhaps the beginning of a new era. Two of the club's loyalists, Trevor Brooking and Frank Lampard, had both gone into retirement, and although Billy Bonds was still on the staff, he was now 39 and feeling his age. Because of a troublesome toe injury – at one time he feared he might have to have it amputated – he hadn't played for nearly a year. He had made a record 624 League appearances for West Ham, and I guessed his first-team days were probably over. But you could never be sure with Bill, such was his determination and level of general fitness. I was delighted to learn in March that he was making yet another comeback in a reserve match against Chelsea.

By this time, Everton had a comfortable lead at the top of the First Division, but because of the disruption to the fixtures caused by the bad weather, we had played four games less than them. Manchester United, who had led by ten points when they knocked us out of the Milk Cup in

October, were now in second place, four points behind Everton.

Having beaten Charlton Athletic and Ipswich Town in the earlier rounds, West Ham were now due to face United in the fifth round of the FA Cup at Upton Park. Ron Atkinson's team were, of course, the FA Cup holders, having beaten Everton the previous May in the final at Wembley. McAvennie put us in front, and although United suffered the misfortune of losing their captain, Bryan Robson, after only three minutes, they staged a spirited comeback in the second half and earned a replay with a goal from Frank Stapleton after seventy-three minutes. So we went to Old Trafford, where we had been knocked out of the FA Cup in two of the previous three seasons.

The game provided one of my happiest memories of the season – a bullet of a header from Geoff Pike. He was outside the penalty area when he connected with Mark Ward's corner in the eighteenth minute. I was delighted for him. He was one of our unsung heroes that season. Ray Stewart, by this time quite remarkably cool and consistent with his penalties, secured a 2–0 win from the spot.

We had only three days to recover from that game before facing Sheffield Wednesday in the sixth round at Hillsborough. Wednesday led 2–0 at half-time, and although McAvennie set up a chance for Cottee soon after the interval, we never really got back into the game. I was a little concerned. Liverpool now led the First Division, and although they had ten points more than us, we had played four games fewer. I considered the Championship a realistic target, but the end-of-season fixture congestion was going to be an extra burden for us. The players had looked tired against Sheffield

Wednesday. Were they going to be strong enough to sustain a challenge for the title?

The answer, when it finally came, was emphatic, but I had a troubled few days first. Immediately after that Wednesday defeat, we lost 1–0 at Arsenal and 2–1 at Aston Villa, two costly set-backs. Then, three days after the Villa defeat, McAvennie rediscovered his touch and scored against Wednesday to give us a 1–0 win at Upton Park and avenge our FA Cup exit. It was his twenty-second goal of the season. We had thirteen matches still to play, and the fixture schedule dictated that we play them in thirty-seven days – approximately three games a week until the end of the season.

By the middle of April, Cottee and McAvennie were brilliantly in tune again, and when we faced Newcastle at Upton Park we needed a win to lift us into third place. More than 24,000 fans flocked to Upton Park that Monday night, sensing perhaps that, for the first time in the club's history, we might win the League title. It was a memorable evening, and some of our football was breathtaking. We beat Newcastle 8–1 but, to be fair, I have to point out that they used three different goalkeepers that night. Their regular first-choice goalkeeper, Martin Thomas, started the match with a shoulder injury, and the only reason he played was because his deputy, David McKellar, was suffering with a hip injury. Thomas was obviously in pain and left the field after forty-six minutes, to be replaced by the little Northern Ireland striker, Ian Stewart. As the goals flew in, Newcastle manager Willie McFaul finally decided to replace him, too, with Peter Beardsley.

I felt sorry for them in their predicament, but we were chasing the Championship and needed the goals to boost our

goal difference. Alvin Martin, an inspiring centre half throughout the season and now captain as successor to Billy Bonds,
scored the first and only hat-trick of his career. McAvennie,
Neil Orr, Ray Stewart, Paul Goddard, who came on as an
eightieth-minute substitute, and an own goal from Newcastle's
Glenn Roeder, gave us our most emphatic win of the season.
We were now third behind the Merseyside giants, Liverpool
and Everton, both of whom had played more games than us.
And, despite that 8–1 win, we still had an inferior goal
difference. There were five games left to play.

West Ham's last five games spanned just ten days – a
demanding schedule and hardly the fairest way to settle a
nine-month-long Championship race. Most daunting of all,
the final match was against defending champions Everton at
Goodison Park, a game that could have settled the Championship. The players knew precisely what was at stake. Lengthy
team talks weren't necessary. They just wanted to get on
with it. None of them had won a League Championship
medal before.

Five days after the Newcastle match, we beat relegation-
threatened Coventry City 1–0 at Upton Park, the predatory
Cottee supplying the goal. Two days later we beat Manchester
City 1–0 with a Ray Stewart penalty. When we played our
third Championship match at Upton Park in five days,
against Ipswich Town, more than 31,000 squeezed into the
ground. Back in February, on a frozen night at Portman
Road, we had knocked Ipswich out of the FA Cup, so I
knew they would be seeking their revenge.

For a few minutes I thought they might get it, when
Kevin Wilson gave them the lead in the sixty-third minute.
But the strength of character within the West Ham team,

epitomized by Alvin Martin's driving performance, provided the base for our revival. Alan Dickens equalized in the seventy-third minute, and Ray Stewart secured a 2–1 victory with his ninth penalty of the season.

The other results were as important as our own that evening. Liverpool beat Leicester 2–0 to maintain their lead, and second-placed Everton lost 1–0 at Oxford, and with that defeat went any chance they had of retaining the title. We were third, four points behind Liverpool, whose final game was against Chelsea at Stamford Bridge. We had two games still to play – six points at stake. If we won our last two games and Liverpool failed to beat Chelsea, West Ham would win the League Championship for the first time, and I would achieve a career-long ambition.

The club programme for the Ipswich match that evening included a photograph of Tony Cottee, Frank McAvennie and Mark Ward receiving their 'Player of the Year' awards. Tony, who had already won the Professional Footballers' Association award for Young Player of the Year, had been voted number one by the Hammers' fans. Frank was second and Mark third. With typical modesty, Tony sought to underline his good playing relationship with Frank, when he was quoted in the accompanying article:

'I felt Frank deserved it more than me. He has come down from Scotland and generated so much interest in the club.'

On 3 May we played West Bromwich Albion, already relegated, at the Hawthorns, and Liverpool played their final game at Stamford Bridge. It was a Saturday afternoon, and the West Ham fans on the Albion terraces were glued to their transistor radios for news from Stamford Bridge. As sometimes happens on these occasions, a rumour swept round the ground just before half-time suggesting that Chelsea were leading. I ignored it.

McAvennie and Cottee struck with the customary precision in the opening twenty-five minutes, and when we went into the dressing room at half-time we were leading 2–1. The real news from Stamford Bridge was not so good, though. Liverpool were leading 1–0, the goalscorer Kenny Dalglish. We eventually beat Albion 3–2 but Liverpool held on to their 1–0 lead, took three points off Chelsea in front of 44,000 fans and, for us, became uncatchable. Liverpool were the League Champions for a record sixteenth time, and seven days later they beat Everton 3–1 at Wembley to clinch the fabled League and FA Cup 'double'. It was a remarkable first season for Dalglish as player-manager. Some were surprised when he succeeded Joe Fagan, but he proved that season that, whether playing or managing or both, he had a remarkable gift for winning. Apart from everything else, he won his 100th cap for Scotland that season. Few people know that as a youngster in Glasgow he came to West Ham for a week's training. He was homesick, though, and chose to join Celtic.

It wasn't the first time that Liverpool had been an unbreachable obstacle at some significant stage in my managerial career. And it wouldn't be the last.

So a sense of anti-climax hung over the team as we went to Goodison Park for the final game that would decide who finished runners-up to Liverpool. Five days before the FA Cup Final against their great Merseyside rivals, Everton beat us 3–1, Gary Lineker scoring twice to take his total for the season to thirty goals. That, plus his performance a month later with England in the 1986 World Cup in Mexico, clinched his fabulous transfer to Terry Venables's Barcelona.

Our goal that night was scored by Cottee, taking his total for the season to twenty-six in all first-team competitions. McAvennie had scored twenty-eight so, at least, that partnership had proved fruitful.

We'd won eight of our last ten matches, and it was disappointing for me, and the players, to have come so close to the title. We had finished third, the highest placing in the club's history, and we had done it with some style. That was satisfying, but the football man's dream is the League Championship. To sustain a challenge over forty-two games, as it was then, against the best teams in the country, is the pinnacle of achievement in the game. It is a prize only a few have lifted. Most managers can spend a lifetime in the game and not get close. At least I got close.

THE LAST SEASON

In May 1987, Tony Cottee handed West Ham a written transfer request. I wasn't surprised, but I was disappointed. He had been outstanding throughout 1986–7, finishing leading scorer with twenty-nine goals, but the team as a whole had performed indifferently. After finishing third the previous season I was nursing hopes of again sustaining a challenge for the First Division title, but it didn't materialize. Tony, an ambitious young man, had earned a place in Bobby Robson's England squad, and he felt that a move to a superleague-type club might enhance his international prospects.

His goalscoring had been one of the few consistent features of 1986–7 and I considered him an invaluable member of the first team. We had started the season encouragingly, with a 1–0 home win against Coventry and a spectacular 3–2 win over Manchester United at Old Trafford – Frank McAvennie scoring twice – two days later. By the time we faced Chelsea at Upton Park in October, we were fifth in the table. That was one of the most enthralling matches of the season. We lost McAvennie with a hamstring injury at half-time, and I replaced him, much to the delight of the crowd, with 40-year-old Billy Bonds. We were trailing 3–2 with thirty minutes to go, but won 5–3, Cottee scoring two of our goals.

At the end of November, when we travelled to play

Newcastle at St James' Park, we were the only First Division side yet to lose an away game. I was beginning to think that we might, indeed, be challenging for the title at the end of the season. Newcastle were near the bottom of the table and clearly had other ideas. They dismantled us that day, quite thoroughly, and Peter Beardsley was our chief tormentor, assisted by the former West Ham favourite Paul Goddard, who went off in the second half with an eye injury. We paticularly wanted to make a good impression to show that the previous season's third place was no flash in the pan, because the match was televised, but they beat us 4–0.

From that moment, nothing much went right. I lost Ray Stewart with injury against Newcastle, and he didn't play again for three months. Shortly after that I also lost our two centre backs, Tony Gale and Alvin Martin, and then Alan Devonshire – all injured. The position with injuries was critical, so, more because of circumstances than design, I went into the transfer market and signed two defenders, Gary Strodder from Lincoln for £100,000, and Tommy McQueen from Aberdeen for £100,000. I remembered, too, a chance meeting I'd had with Stewart Robson a few weeks earlier. After West Ham had drawn 0–0 with Arsenal at Highbury – a morning kick-off – I travelled to Upton Park to watch the reserve fixture against Arsenal in the afternoon. Stewart played for Arsenal reserves that day, and when I arrived at the ground he was in the dressing room sitting in the bath, nursing an injury. I asked him what was wrong and he told me he had a recurring groin problem. He feared it might need surgery, and subsequently he had a hernia operation. Because of our injuries and our poor results that Christmas, I decided that we needed his forceful type of player in midfield.

I admired his industry and appetite for the game. He was a box-to-box player who, like his friend Tony Cottee, had just got into the England squad and was being talked of as the next Bryan Robson. A strong, upright lad and a former Brentwood public schoolboy, I thought he would be an ideal signing for West Ham. I asked George Graham, the Arsenal manager, if he was prepared to sell him, and when he said that he was, he quickly pointed out that, not long before, he'd had a hernia operation. We agreed a £640,000 fee and had a gentleman's agreement with Arsenal that if Stewart failed to establish his full match-fitness they would take him back to Highbury. His medical examination at West Ham was extensive and, our medical staff having satisfied themselves that he was fit, he made his debut in a 3–1 win at Coventry in January.

We won only six more games in Division One that season, and even the arrival of another Arsenal old boy, Liam Brady, couldn't halt the slide. I signed Brady from the Italian club Ascoli in March 1987, for £80,000, one of the easiest transfers to negotiate throughout my time at Upton Park. After we made our initial approaches, Liam came to my house.

'I admire the way you play at West Ham,' he said. 'I'd like to sign for you.'

He was a refreshing player to deal with. Talking personal terms with him was a pleasure and couldn't have been simpler. Obviously his years in Italian football had made him financially secure, but even so, I liked the way he said: 'Pay me whatever you consider I'm worth without upsetting the wage scale at the club.'

He was a joy to watch and a joy to work with, and his experience both at home and in Italy made him a valuable acquisition. He was so beautifully balanced and deft of touch, that I often felt he could peel a grape with his left foot, so complete was his mastery of the ball. I was delighted when he scored his first goal for the club in our 3–1 win against Arsenal at Upton Park in April. Cottee hit the other two in what was one of our few convincing victories in the second half of the season. We finished fifteenth in the First Division.

The abrupt reversal in form was obviously in Tony Cottee's mind when he asked for a transfer. Like all good young players, he wanted to win trophies, and once again we had blown our chance. In the eight weeks following his transfer request, I didn't receive a single enquiry from another club for him. When he called me at home during the summer, I told him this and suggested he come round one afternoon for a talk. We sat in the garden and talked for three hours. I told him it hadn't been an easy season for any of us. I told him quite definitely that he should go away, settle down and work at his game. He accepted my advice.

Sadly, the next season, 1987–8, couldn't have started worse. We lost 3–0 at home to Queen's Park Rangers, and after sixty minutes Alan Devonshire limped off with an achilles' tendon injury that later required surgery. He didn't play again that season. We won only three of our first fifteen matches, and by November we were in fifteenth place in the table. Little items kept appearing in the newspapers suggesting that Tony Cottee was unhappy at Upton Park and, worse still, Frank McAvennie had decided he wanted to return to Scotland and play for Celtic.

Frank was a Glasgow boy and made it clear on the first day we met that he had been a Celtic fan since childhood. His ambition, he told me, was to wear those famous green and white hooped shirts. I knew that when I signed him; he was totally honest with me about it. When Celtic began their search for a new striker early in 1987–8, Frank was linked regularly with them in the newspapers. When the Celtic manager, Billy McNeill, contacted me and asked if West Ham would release McAvennie, I felt I had a duty to tell the player. I had told him that if Celtic ever made an official approach I would tell him. I didn't want to lose him, but I didn't feel I could deny him the chance to fulfil an ambition. Apart from that I have always believed that it was senseless having an unhappy player on the staff. Celtic were prepared to pay £725,000 for him. He wanted to realize his ambition, and we couldn't stand in his way. The deal was completed.

I was very sorry to lose him and, in many ways, he was sorry to go. He had struck up a great rapport with the Upton Park crowd and had become one of the most popular players of recent years. For me, he was an outstanding professional, on and off the field. He enjoyed the bright lights and spent a lot of his spare time with Arsenal's Charlie Nicholas, who had risen to superstardom in London. Like Charlie, Frank was much in demand as a celebrity, but he knew how to handle his fame.

He was always at Chadwell Heath each morning, ready for training, and on the rare occasion he was late his hand would be dipping into his pocket for the customary £5 fine as he made his apologies. He was an easy person to deal with, forthright and good natured, and if he felt something wasn't going right with his game he would come and talk to me about it. His departure was a big loss, just at the time I thought we might be getting a settled squad together.

I knew he would be a very difficult player to replace. No

club wants to lose quality strikers, and those that were prepared to even listen to offers were asking astronomical prices. Until I could find a suitable replacement, I reorganized the side. I decided to take Alan Dickens out of midfield and play him just behind Cottee, rather as Spurs had done with Glenn Hoddle before selling him to Monaco. It was a short-term move, just as my decision to play Paul Ince in a sweeper role had been a few weeks earlier. With Tony Gale recovering from an achilles' injury, the defence had looked vulnerable early in the season and I felt Ince would give us a little extra balance and depth at the back. He was such a comfortable player on the ball that I knew he would adapt to the task, but like most systems it has its weaknesses as well as its strengths. Obviously, we sacrificed some attacking momentum. We simply weren't getting enough players forward. Paul, yet to fulfil his enormous potential, was already a richly talented player, who would have been as valuable in attack as defence. His only problem at that time was his stamina. He was just 20, and I've always believed that there is no point in running youngsters into the ground over forty games. Even so, he played twenty-six games in the First Division that season and now, of course, has developed into a much stronger player.

The Christmas period was disastrous for us, with successive defeats against Wimbledon, Tottenham and Norwich.

Typical of Alan Dickens, he sacrificed his own game to fill an unfamiliar role at the front, but it was clear that Cottee missed the benefit of having a natural striker like McAvennie alongside him. I knew I would have to invest in another striker. I first tried for Mick Harford of Luton Town. Vastly experienced, he was 28 years old, and although I had much respect for his ability I still had to decide whether he would be a good investment for the club. Luton wanted £1 million for him. I decided we should try to sign him, but he wasn't sure that he wanted to join us and, that apart, he was suffering with an ankle injury. I told him to think about it, but by the time he had recovered from the injury Luton were through to the fifth round of the Littlewoods Cup – they went on to beat Arsenal at Wembley – and he didn't want to leave.

I then tried for another striker on the fringe of the England squad, Kerry Dixon of Chelsea. Like us, Chelsea were under pressure near the bottom of the table, but Kerry, who struck me as a very amiable individual, could see few advantages in a move to Upton Park at that time. Remember, too, that Arsenal were interested in him. He eventually said no and later decided to stay at Stamford Bridge. After talking it over with my chief scout, Eddie Baily, we decided to switch our search away from the strikers with experience and pedigree to those in the highly promising category. Top among these, in my opinion, was Leroy Rosenior. A little over six feet, strong as a bull and sure of touch, Leroy, I felt, could supplement Tony's goals and get us out of trouble. He'd proved that he could score goals in the Fist Division during a brief spell with Queen's Park Rangers. He was now back at Fulham and I asked them how much they wanted for him. The fee was £290,000, the negotiations with Leroy and his wife were uncomplicated, and he signed for us just before the March transfer deadline.

He became an immediate favourite with the fans at Upton Park by scoring on his debut in a 1–0 win over Watford, the club he turned down to join us. It was an important win for us that March, but disastrous for Watford, who were sinking deeper into trouble at the foot of the table.

I felt sorry for them, because I have admired what the club has achieved during Elton John's reign as chairman. I saw him standing alone in the corridor outside the dressing rooms about ninety minutes before the game, and I thought he needed a bit of cheering up. I'd met him several times and knew him to be a very amiable man. I invited him into my office for a cup of tea.

'No, John. You've got enough to do. Thanks all the same,' he said. But I insisted and he came and joined me for a chat. We talked for about fifteen minutes. I assumed he was concerned about the club's position, and he was, but he had other things on his mind, too. We talked about football and our lives away from the game. We discussed our problems, and I think we both felt grateful for the chat.

I thought no more of it, but the following Christmas a case of champagne arrived at the club, addressed to me. The attached note read: 'Thanks for the chat. Elton.' It was a total surprise, but a typical gesture from a generous man.

By that time, of course, Watford were in Division Two, but Leroy's goal had played a major role in securing our First Division status. He scored four more goals after the Watford match, most significantly two against Chelsea in a 4–1 win in our final home match.

Chelsea had just one point more than us at the time, were unbeaten in their previous four games, and knew that defeat at Upton Park would put their own First Division place in serious jeopardy. For our part, the season-long plague of injuries had shown no sign of easing, and we faced Chelsea without experienced first-team men like Ray Stewart, Alvin Martin, Alan Devonshire and Liam Brady.

The attendance was 28,521, the second biggest of the season at Upton Park, and Leroy, the new local hero, gave them plenty to shout about with his two goals in the opening thirty-seven minutes. The other two were provided by Paul Hilton and Cottee, once again finishing the season as the club's leading marksman. This time, though, he scored only thirteen goals, his lowest total for five seasons.

Those three points virtually ensured our survival in Division One. Our last game was against Newcastle at St James' Park, and we had to lose by six goals to be relegated on goal difference. Tom McAlister had enjoyed an outstanding season in goal, missing only one match, but I took no chances against Newcastle. Phil Parkes, who had spent most of the season either in the reserves or on the treatment table, travelled with us, and I took the precaution of putting him on the substitute's bench, just in case Tom was injured. My thoughts went back to the misfortune suffered by Newcastle when they had to use three goalkeepers because of injuries – and we beat them 8–1. This time we lost 2–1 but at least we were safe again. We finished sixteenth and shared forty-two points with two other London clubs – Chelsea and Charlton. Chelsea had the worst goal difference; they finished eighteenth, in the play-off place, and were subsequently relegated to Division Two.

We had avoided the drop, but only just. Injuries are a constant problem for all managers, but we had been particularly unlucky. Tony Cottee was the only player to have appeared in all forty First Division matches that season, and he was about to leave. He wanted to go, and, if we were offered the right money, I decided I would recommend to the board that we release him.

For most of the season I had insisted that Tony wasn't for sale at any price. But a few months earlier, a great personal friend, Reg Drury, the football correspondent of the *News of the World*, had asked what I would accept for him. As a result of that conversation, I read in the *News of the World* the following Sunday that West Ham would only consider offers of more than £2 million for Cottee, if we decided to sell him at the end of the season. Soon after that story appeared, Colin Harvey, the Everton manager, called me and said that he was interested in buying Cottee. I confirmed what had appeared in the newspaper: we would want at least £2 million and we wouldn't consider any business until the end of the season.

The Everton chairman, Philip Carter, spoke to Mr Len and offered £1.75 million. I recommended to the board that we turn it down. 'We must get £2 million,' I insisted, and the board agreed.

Everton returned and paid a club-record £2 million net. By this time, of course, Arsenal were also interested. Tony spoke to both clubs and then made his decision to move to Goodison Park.

I had lost two top-class strikers but had to accept that players of the quality of McAvennie and Cottee would always attract the interest of the superleague-type clubs. I could understand the players wanting the financial security and the promise of success that these clubs offer. It was our loss – mine, the club's and the supporters' – but it struck me as ironic that we rarely acknowledge that other clubs probably feel the same sense of loss when we sign one of their big-name players.

I used some of the money from Tony's transfer to buy

David Kelly from Walsall for £600,000 and Allen McKnight from Celtic for £250,000. Kelly was a lively, athletic striker, who had already played for the Republic of Ireland, and the fact that Spurs, Bayern Munich and Paris St Germain were also interested underlined his status in the game as a goalscorer of enormous potential. Although McKnight was the regular first-choice goalkeeper for Northern Ireland, he was understudy to Pat Bonner at Celtic. He did so well when deputizing for Bonner in first-team matches that I believed he might develop sufficiently to be a long-term successor to Phil Parkes.

In the space of three seasons, the squad had changed considerably. We had lost an entire front line in Goddard, McAvennie and Cottee. Neil Orr had gone, Billy Bonds had retired and Phil Parkes was approaching his 39th birthday. We now faced the task of blending several new faces, like Kelly, Rosenior and McKnight, with other recent signings like Robson, Brady and Julian Dicks, a competitive left back signed from Birmingham City for £300,000 in March 1988. It was a period of transition, once again severely disrupted by injuries.

Purely by coincidence, during that summer of 1988 West Ham received some literature from the National Coaching Foundation, informing us of a series of lectures they were organizing at the West London Institute on endurance, power, speed and diet for professional sportsmen. It was an area I was interested in, particularly in view of the team's run of injuries in the previous two seasons.

I attended two of the lectures with the West Ham coaches Mick McGiven and Ronnie Boyce. We were so impressed with what we heard that we thought it was an area we should explore more fully. I contacted the organizing physiologist involved with the lectures, Angela Cannell, and asked if she could give us some guidance on our pre-season training schedules. She said she would, and she also recruited her colleague John Brierley, a former British international triple jumper, to help us. He was a superb athlete, a speed and power man. Together with their staff they carried out various tests on the players to determine how we could improve their fitness and enhance their recovery rate when they were injured. If a player lacked stamina, it showed in the tests. If he lacked speed, that showed, too. They examined the players' diets, and some players, notably Paul Ince and Kevin Keen, two lightweights, were advised to change their eating habits.

It wasn't simply a case of eating the wrong food, but of eating at the wrong time. A lot of players don't like to eat first thing in the morning, because they have to train. For some players, though, it is better to eat in the morning, otherwise, like Keen and Ince, they dehydrate during training and therefore don't function properly.

As a physiologist, Angela was an expert on what makes the body work. She knew how the body should function, just like a mechanic knows how a car should function. Her rehabilitation work with the players during my last season was invaluable. For me, she solved the problem of the grey area between the physiotherapist and resumption of full training. When an injured player finally leaves the treatment room, he is not always ready to resume full training. As the treatment room had been full every day for two years, I couldn't expect our physiotherapist, Rob Jenkins, to organize the rehabilitation work as well. He was simply too busy. Angela filled that gap.

Even so, injuries littered the 1988–9 season. We were

without Ray Stewart and Stewart Robson for most of the season. Liam Brady and Alan Devonshire each missed half of the season through injury. Alvin Martin, Tony Gale and Mark Ward all missed a considerable number of games and, after his return, Frank McAvennie pulled a hamstring and we lost him for four vital games at the end of the season. These are not excuses. These are facts – the reality of football.

The omens were bad on the opening day of the season, when we were comprehensively beaten 4–0 at Southampton. I had to make two changes at half-time because of injuries. Tony Gale had strained a calf muscle, and the young striker Stuart Slater had blood pouring from an ear after taking a heavy bang on the head early in the game. It was not the ideal way to start the season.

Worse was to come. Our first home game was against Charlton Athletic, who'd made a habit of securing unexpected results at Upton Park. We made a special occasion of the match for Billy Bonds, who had announced his retirement and was now installed as youth team coach. He had started his career with Charlton, before moving to West Ham and making 794 first-team appearances. We gathered four players who spanned his career in the game – Brian Kinsey, from Bill's days at the Valley, and three from West Ham: Geoff Hurst, Frank Lampard and Patsy Holland. They presented him with a framed montage of photographs depicting his career.

Half an hour later I was wishing I still had him in the team. Paul Williams, the tricky little former Woodford Town striker, scored for Charlton in the twenty-first and forty-eighth minutes, and although Kevin Keen pulled a goal back from the penalty spot, Charlton won 3–1 after Stewart Robson unfortunately scored an own goal.

So, in our opening two matches, we had suffered two heavy defeats and conceded seven goals. It wasn't good enough. We needed to stabilize and restore some confidence. Tom McAlister, who had been a faithful understudy to Phil Parkes in goal for seven years, played in those first two games. I decided to leave him out of the side and, as it turned out, they were the last League games he played for the club. I brought in Allen McKnight for his debut against Wimbledon at Plough Lane – quite a formidable prospect for a new goalkeeper, considering Wimbledon's belligerent style of play and their reliance on the long ball into the penalty area. Allen was equal to the challenge, refused to be intimidated by John Fashanu, and caught all the high balls. A Mark Ward goal gave us a 1–0 win.

The relief I felt was fleeting. After a 2–2 draw against Aston Villa at Upton Park, we lost four consecutive matches, and by the middle of October we were in twentieth place, at the foot of the table. What I found most disconcerting was our lack of consistency. We seemed able to rise to the challenge for the Cup ties, but our form in the First Division matches was lamentable.

We beat Sunderland 3–0 at Roker Park in the first leg of the Littlewoods Cup second round – David Kelly scoring twice – and followed that with a 2–1 win in the second leg, Kelly again scoring. In the third round we were drawn at home to Derby County. It was the beginning of November, and they were fifth in the First Division. Our indifferent start meant that only 14,226 turned up for the game – and those that didn't missed a treat. We thrashed Derby 5–0, with Paul Ince playing an influential role in midfield. He was now a regular in the side and playing exceptionally well in a central midfield role in the absence of Stewart Robson.

After just seven games it had been obvious that Robson wouldn't be able to continue. His last game was in a 4–1 defeat against his old club, Arsenal, at Upton Park. He sat in the dressing room at the end complaining of soreness in the groin. It had been a problem for him since the start of the season, and we decided that he should consult a specialist and, if necessary, have surgery to rectify the problem. Some weeks after that he had a pelvic operation, and a year later he was sadly still unable to play.

Our League form remained indifferent throughout November, but at least we managed to climb off the bottom of the table. Then, on the last day of the month, we met Liverpool at Upton Park in the fourth round of the Littlewoods Cup.

Liverpool were, of course, the League Champions, but at that time they were having problems similar to our own, though with a squad as strong as theirs they were able to patch over the cracks more successfully. They were sixth in the table but, most significantly, were without a handful of key players because of injury – Bruce Grobbelaar, Gary Gillespie, Alan Hansen, John Barnes and Ian Rush. Steve McMahon, who had been injured, returned to face us. The point is that when they were all fit and back in the side, Liverpool were able to string together nineteen matches in the second half of the season with just one defeat – the Championship decider against Arsenal in the final game. Even a team like Liverpool falters when the best and most experienced players are ruled out.

Even so, on the night we played them they paraded players like Steve Nichol, Peter Beardsley, Ray Houghton, Ronnie Whelan and Steve McMahon. We were fortunate enough to have Brady and Devonshire fit and together in the side for the first time that season. They masterminded our 4–1 victory. It was Liverpool's heaviest defeat in a domestic cup competition for fifty years. Because of another injury to Mark Ward, I played Devonshire wide on the right, the first time he had played out there for nine years. He was magnificent, setting up attacking opportunities and closing down space, too. The old heads, his and Liam's, helped the youngsters secure one of the most memorable Cup victories of my time at West Ham. The fans applauded both teams off the field at the end, and that night I think we saw the emergence of a new young star – Paul Ince. He scored twice, refused a TV interview after the match, and went home quietly. From that moment on, the bigger clubs began taking notice of Ince.

I was delighted with our performance that night, and three days later we went to play Millwall at the Den in a First Division match. Newly promoted, they were unbeaten at home, third in the table and sweeping all before them. It was one of the few occasions that season when I was able to retain an unchanged team. We worked hard and defended stoutly, and the persistence of Alan Dickens in midfield set up the only goal. The scorer was Ince.

I sensed we were beginning to rediscover our confidence, but, to be really sure, I knew we had to survive unbeaten for five or six games. The next match was a goalless draw at home to Sheffield Wednesday, and then suddenly it all began to turn sour again. We lost to Spurs, Norwich and Wimbledon and drew with Charlton over the Christmas and New Year holiday programmes. The one bonus was that when Devonshire dropped out injured, Ray Stewart was fit to return to the side. He played at centre back for two games, but when we faced Arsenal at Upton Park in the third round of the FA Cup in January, I installed him in his natural position at right back.

We held Arsenal to a 2–2 draw, and three days later went to Highbury for the replay. Our away form had been more impressive than our home form, so I wasn't too concerned about playing at Highbury. Even so, the bookies' odds were 7 to 1 against a West Ham victory. The last team to have beaten Arsenal in an FA Cup replay at Highbury were West Bromwich Albion, and that was back in 1957. It was a tight, uncompromising match, settled when Alan Dickens chipped the ball into the Arsenal penalty area. While several Arsenal defenders hesitated, Leroy Rosenior nipped in at the back post to head his fifth goal of the season, and secure a 1–0 victory.

Again we followed a good Cup win with an encouraging result in the League – and again it was away from home. This time we won 2–1 at Derby County's Baseball Ground, with Kelly and Brady scoring the goals. Our problem, in the League at least, was playing at Upton Park. By March we had won only once at home in Division One – against Newcastle back in October. It had become a psychological hurdle for us, and the understandable frustration of the Upton Park fans wasn't helping. The home team is expected to win the home matches – and we were losing ours. But the pattern of the game has changed in the last few years, and the reward of three points for a win has encouraged more teams to attack away from home. Visiting sides were happy to get players behind the ball at Upton Park, deny us time and space, and hope to hit us on the break. Many teams are now so well organized in all parts of the field that they are able to play a containing game for the full ninety minutes. The longer the game progresses, the more risks the home side takes in an effort to break the stranglehold. The more risks they take, the more vulnerable they become at the back. And, of course, the home-team players sense the frustration of the crowd, and this provokes them into areas of even greater risk.

Several teams last season enjoyed better results away than at home. The table opposite illustrates how much the game has changed in this respect. To make the comparison between the two seasons clearer, the points column in the 1988–9 part of the table assumes two points for a win, rather than the three that are now awarded. It should be remembered, however, that in 1988–9 only thirty-eight games were played, whereas forty-two were played in 1978–9.

Even so, in ten years the swing has been quite remarkable. Last season West Ham, for instance, won only three home League games, the lowest number in the club's history. But we won seven away matches. In the game of a few years ago such statistics would have appeared illogical, if not impossible. But that is how the game has developed, and West Ham, like every other team, has to adapt to the new challenges. Last season we struggled to cope with visiting teams at Upton Park. As the season unfolded, the players inevitably felt increasing pressure. I could understand the frustration of the supporters. We were winning our Cup matches at home, but losing the League matches and jeopardizing our First Division status.

A classic example of our inconsistency came in the space of three days, late in January. We attracted 30,110 to Upton Park for our Littlewoods Cup fifth-round tie against Aston Villa. The injury situation was still bleak. I was without

THE LAST SEASON

1988–9

	Home wins	Total home points	Away wins	Total away points
Top four				
Arsenal	10	26	12	28
Liverpool	11	27	11	27
Nottm Forest	8	23	9	24
Norwich	8	23	9	22
Bottom two				
West Ham	3	12	7	16
Newcastle	3	12	4	12

1978–9

	Home wins	Total home points	Away wins	Total away points
Top four				
Liverpool	19	40	11	28
Nottm Forest	11	32	10	28
WBA	13	31	6	28
Everton	12	31	5	20
Bottom two				
Birmingham	5	19	1	3
Chelsea	3	11	2	9

Alvin Martin, and the week before, in that 2–1 win at Derby, Ray Stewart had been stretchered off with a knee injury that eventually required surgery. He didn't play again that season.

I had to reorganize the team again to face Villa, but I had one bonus. A few weeks earlier our physiologist, Angela Cannell, had joined the club on a full-time basis. One of her first tasks was to get Mark Ward match fit. He had been out of action since November, and I didn't expect to have him back in the first-team squad until February at the earliest. When Angela arrived she worked with Mark every day for a fortnight. On the morning of the Villa match, he came into my office and said: 'I'm fit. I think I can play.'

I was a little dubious. He hadn't even played a reserve match. I spoke to Angela and she said: 'As far as I'm concerned he's available for selection.'

I put him on the substitute's bench against Villa. He came on for Alan Dickens early in the second half and helped us win 2–1 and clinch a place against Luton Town in the semi-finals of the Littlewoods Cup.

Three days after that match, an Upton Park crowd of 29,822 saw us lose 3–1 to Manchester United. Inexplicable!

A week later we drew 0–0 at Swindon – Lou Macari's Second Division team – in the fourth round of the FA Cup. A Leroy Rosenior goal gave West Ham a 1–0 victory in the replay – at Upton Park. I was delighted with our progress in the two domestic knockout competitions, but growing increasingly concerned at our position in the First Division table. At the beginning of February we were bottom of the table with Newcastle. Both teams had seventeen points. Sheffield Wednesday were above us – six points clear.

Relegation was a very real threat, though we still had

sixteen games in which to get out of trouble. I had no need to stress to the players what relegation would mean to them as individuals and to the club as a whole. It can mean significantly less finance to any relegated club, but we were fortunate that season in that we played fourteen major cup ties, probably netting the club around £1 million in revenue. Usually, of course, the loss of First Division status automatically means less money for the players, less for transfers and, in some cases, staff cuts. I told the players regularly that they were playing for each other. Each was as responsible for the future of other members of the team as he was for himself.

As for myself, I had a contract that expired in June 1989. I realized that relegation would do little to enhance my own prospects. In previous years, a few months before a contract expired, I would be discussing terms with Mr Len. On this occasion, because of our position in the table and the mounting problems with injuries, we had agreed to leave any talks until the end of the season. We did this at my suggestion. I never sensed that my position was under threat. All the members of the board were amicable and cooperative, just as they had always been. I felt my priority was to get the team settled and playing well again. My own future could wait until the end of the season.

I believed we were good enough to climb out of trouble, and I also believed we could get to Wembley in the Littlewoods Cup – and maybe even the FA Cup. In the middle of February we had two important games – the first leg of the Littlewoods Cup semifinal against Luton at Upton Park, followed by a visit to Charlton Athletic in the fifth round of the FA Cup. I was fortunate in that I had Martin, Gale, Brady and Devonshire all fit; Ward was now back in the side as well. A tough, unyielding character, he had the sort of spirit we would need in the coming weeks.

I made the training as competitive as I dared, hoping that the fighting instinct would ingrain itself in the players and re-emerge in match situations. Little Mark Ward relished that combative atmosphere, both in training and on the playing field.

One morning, during a particularly hectic session of 'keep ball' in the gymnasium at Chadwell Heath, I wandered foolishly from my usual position on the sidelines into the heat of the battle, to have a quiet word with a YTS boy. At times I had to use several of the youngsters to make up the numbers in training, and often the speed the ball moved at was something they simply couldn't cope with. Whenever the ball arrived at this lad's feet, it was whipped away from him before he could play it. I weaved a path through the play to the middle of the gym to talk to him.

I was standing with my back to the play, telling the lad what he should do, when, without any warning, I was literally lifted several feet off the floor. I fell heavily and lay on the ground, stunned, thinking that at the very least I'd been hit by a buffalo. They play stopped and the lads stood around with sheepish grins.

'Sorry, John,' said Mark Ward. 'I didn't see you. Are you alright?'

I was far from alright. As the lads picked me up off the ground I realized I had hurt my knee, the left knee that had forced me to retire as a player. I was in agony. As I hopped out of the gym to the treatment room, I couldn't understand how a little guy like Ward, 5 feet 6 inches and barely 10 stone, could pack enough power to lift me off the ground and inflict so much damage.

Rob Jenkins, the club's physiotherapist, told me the knee was twisted, but in the circumstances there was no chance of taking a few days off to rest it. The following morning I limped into the training ground. I had a pressure bandage on the knee, which was still badly swollen.

One of the great strengths of a football team, at least my football team, was the ability we had to share a joke, even in times of crisis. As I sat with my leg propped up on a chair, drinking tea with Rob Jenkins and my coaches, we hatched a little plot that, if nothing else, would brighten the day for the rest of the players.

I went to the treatment room, took off the pressure bandage and pulled on a pair of shorts. Rob encased my leg from thigh to ankle in an inflatable splint, designed to immobilize broken limbs. I then went and sat in a chair with my immobilized leg propped on another chair. I was positioned so that I would be the first person Mark Ward saw when he reported for training that morning.

I sat with two crutches across my lap and quickly rehearsed the script with Ronnie Boyce and Rob Jenkins.

Finally, little Wardie arrived, bright, bubbly and totally unsuspecting. He saw me. He saw the crutches. He saw the inflatable splint. His face dropped, and he lifted both hands to his head.

'Oh, no!' he groaned. 'John, what have I done?'

'*You* . . .!' I cried, 'as for you, you just go and get ready for training!'

'Look, John,' said Ronnie, 'you'll have to go and have it done.'

'Oh, no!' cried Wardie again.

'I'm the manager,' I said, 'I make the decisions.'

Perfectly on cue, Rob Jenkins walked in from the treatment room.

'You might be the manager, but if the surgeon says you have to go in immediately, you have to go in immediately.'

Another cry of despair emerged from Mark.

'Are you still here, Wardie?' I said. 'Go and get changed.'

With head bowed he trudged into the players' changing rooms. None of the others let him in on the joke. He was still sitting there, with his head in his hands, when I limped in briskly like Hopalong Cassidy.

'Morning, Wardie!' I said, cheerfully. 'Time for work.'

A chatterbox by nature, it was the first and only time I'd seen him speechless.

The irony of the situation struck me later that day when I, the manager, hobbling with a knee injury, asked Rob Jenkins, the physiotherapist, how many of the players would be unavailable for the next match. Sometimes his treatment room looked like a clearing station for the wounded after the Battle of the Little Bighorn. It was a fact, though, that there were many occasions when I simply could not announce a team until a couple of hours before kick-off, because I was awaiting the results of late fitness tests. There is invariably a silver lining in these circumstances and, for West Ham, it was the emergence of Paul Ince and Stuart Slater. Had it not been for the injuries, their development might have been delayed a further two years. As it was, they had to play, and they both rose to the challenge magnificently. Ince, a lively, confident player, enjoyed a meteoric rise. I remember him first turning up at Chadwell Heath as an ebullient 13-year-old. I think we helped knock him into shape, and it was his form in 1988–9 that earned him his transfer to Manchester United. I was surprised that United's medical examination revealed that Paul had a groin problem, because there was no evidence of any serious groin condition during his time at Upton Park. Once they had satisfied themselves that he was fit to play, and had negotiated a staggered system of paying the £2 million fee, Paul got his wish and joined the club he had supported from childhood.

Soon after his transfer to Old Trafford, Paul called me at home for a chat.

'With a contract like you've got, the first thing that you should do is go out and buy your mum a £500 dress,' I told him.

'That's a good idea, John,' he said. 'I'll do that.' It was just the reply I wanted to hear.

I hope the move to Old Trafford proves successful for him, because he is a lad who deserves a few breaks. I think he found it difficult at first as a teenager adjusting to the demands of professional football. Unlike my own days as a young player at Upton Park, there are today many more temptations and pressures that teenagers have to cope with. I remember getting a telephone call one day to tell me that Paul had been present at a fracas involving old schoolfriends. There was never any question that Paul would be charged, but a detective came down to Chadwell Heath to talk to me about it. The officer took a very caring attitude. He told him that he was a young man other youngsters wanted to look up to and admire. He made Paul aware of his responsibilities as a well-known young footballer in the public eye. I think the message got home.

By the time we faced the holders, Luton, in the semifinal of the Littlewoods Cup, my knee was feeling better. There were times in that match when I wished I could have gone out and helped the players myself. We lost Brady with an injury after thirty-five minutes, but that was no excuse. We were poor defensively. Luton won 3–0, with goals from Mick Harford, Roy Wegerle and Danny Wilson, and the second leg on the artificial surface at Kenilworth Road suddenly looked a daunting prospect.

We had conceded five goals in two games, and I knew that if we were to have any realistic hope in the relegation fight we would have to reinforce the defence. Allen McKnight had played thirty-three consecutive games, but recent errors had provoked the inevitable reaction from the crowd. He felt uncomfortable playing at Upton Park and asked me to leave him out of the side. All players have bad spells and make mistakes, but goalkeepers are particularly vulnerable, in their isolation, to easy criticism. I decided to leave him out for our next game, an FA Cup fifth-round tie againt Charlton at Selhurst Park, and reinstate Phil Parkes.

Approaching his 39th birthday, Phil had played only one first-team game in almost two seasons. He had been troubled by an elbow injury but that had cleared up and, even if his mobility was not what it was he was still a great goalkeeper. I knew his experience, sense of positioning and confidence would be invaluable. He played splendidly against Charlton, and his handling of the ball generated new confidence throughout the team. The star of the day, though, was a youngster half his age – Stuart Slater, who scored the goal in our 1–0 win. He had played only a handful of first-team games, and this was his debut in an FA Cup tie. I had put him in the side because Rosenior had become our latest injury victim.

Stuart is a wonderfully talented little striker, and a marvellous prospect. When it came to ball-juggling skills, there can be few players to match Slater. He once kept the ball up in the gym at Chadwell Heath 10,000 times. His problem is that he is too unselfish. He had to learn to be like other good strikers and become a little greedy when necessary. He has an inclination to pass to a teammate when he would probably do better to shoot at goal himself. Anyway, I was delighted for him that day at Selhurst Park, when he capitalized on good approach work by Alan Devonshire to score the only goal of the match.

With Rosenior injured and Kelly plagued by indifferent form, a great responsibility fell on young Slater. A 2–0 defeat at Luton in the second leg of the Littlewoods Cup semifinal meant that in seven consecutive games we had scored just three goals. I knew I would have to sign another striker if we were to have any chance of avoiding relegation. We needed the impetus that a goalscorer could provide – and particularly a goalscorer like Frank McAvennie.

Having fulfilled his ambition to play for Celtic, I think he finally realized that he would he happier back in London. He had never sold his house in Romford and was a frequent visitor to West Ham's matches. The fact that he had broken an arm and not been fit to play in the Celtic side finally convinced their manager, Billy McNeill, that he should sell him. Once again, the newspapers were full of speculation, and Frank was repeatedly quoted as saying that, if he returned to England, the club he would most like to play for was West Ham.

I spoke to Billy McNeill, who like myself had not wanted to lose him. However, £1.2 million was a convincing argument in our favour. Celtic gave me permission to speak to him, and Frank came to London with his adviser, Bill McMurdo. The first thing Bill told me when I met them was that Arsenal, then staging a dramatic bid for the League title, also wanted to sign him. That was going to be a hell of a problem for West Ham. Anyway, Eddie Baily, Tom Finn and I talked with Frank and Bill for nearly four hours. We left them shortly before midnight, and they drove off immediately to see the Arsenal manager, George Graham.

The following morning, Bill McMurdo called me and said that they intended talking to Arsenal again that day. I was beginning to think that we were going to lose him to Arsenal. That night we were playing Norwich at Carrow Road in an FA Cup sixth-round replay. I always travelled with the team, but on this occasion I sent the coach away and I sat by the telephone in my office. Shortly after midday I got a call from Bill McMurdo telling me that Frank had decided to rejoin West Ham. I was delighted and particularly impressed with the way Frank had handled himself.

When he had first been a West Ham player, he made no secret of the fact that he had always wanted to play for Celtic. When the opportunity came, he signed for them. When he was a Celtic player, he made no secret of the fact that if he got the chance to go back to England he wanted to play for West Ham again. He was true to his word. He had applied the same set of rules, leaving Celtic, as he had done when he left West Ham. Later that day, as I drove to join the team in Norwich, I asked myself: if I had been impartial, which club would I have advised him to join – West Ham or Arsenal? I couldn't be sure. Had Frank chosen to go to Arsenal I would have understood. They are a great club.

The day ended sadly with a 3–1 defeat at Norwich. We were out of the FA Cup, Alvin Martin was injured again, and we were left now to fight against relegation. But at least we had McAvennie back, and three days later he helped us beat Aston Villa 1–0 at Villa Park, where Ince ran half the length of the pitch and hit an unstoppable shot from twenty-five yards to score, for me, the goal of the season.

With ten games remaining, West Ham were bottom of the table, seven points adrift of Newcastle, but with three games in hand. I knew we could still get out of trouble, if only we could win our remaining home matches. McAvennie's return to Upton Park generated enormous enthusiasm and attracted a 27,265 crowd for the visit of our Littlewoods Cup conquerors, Norwich. We lost 2–0.

We lost 3–0 against Tottenham at White Hart Lane, and then, with Rosenior back to provide a goal, we drew 1–1 against Derby at Upton Park. Then came perhaps the two most significant defeats of the season, against teams, like us, struggling against relegation. Both matches were played at Upton Park. First we faced Middlesbrough. We were without, among others, Martin, Gale and Strodder, all central defenders, and had a makeshift centre-back partnership of Paul Hilton and the young full back Steve Potts. With ten minutes remaining we led 1–0, thanks to a magnificent goal from Kevin Keen. Then a lapse of concentration in defence allowed Bernie Slaven to strike twice in six minutes to give Middlesbrough a 2–1 victory.

Four days later, Southampton beat us 2–1 at Upton Park – a defeat, like all the other results that day, totally over-shadowed by the horrific events at Hillsborough, where ninety-five Liverpool fans died on the terraces in the opening minutes of the FA Cup semifinal against Nottingham Forest.

Such tragedies put the winning and losing of football matches into graphic perspective. For me it was the saddest day in the history of the English game. I was still concerned at our plight at the bottom of the table, but when I sat in the comfort and security of my home that night it didn't seem to matter quite so much. I know that was a common reaction among football people throughout the game. Everyone in the sport shared the same feeling of utter sadness.

At our next home game, against Millwall, the club organized a collection for the Hillsborough Disaster Appeal. We raised £5,765, and the club also made a private contribution. That day we beat Millwall 3–0, only our second home win in the League that season. We followed that with a 2–1 win at Newcastle, a good, solid performance, spoiled only by the injury jinx. McAvennie, who hadn't scored a goal in his eight matches, pulled a hamstring and was to miss the next four games.

Three days later, an Alan Dickens goal secured a 1–0 win over Luton at Upton Park, our third home League win. You could sense the optimism flooding back. At the end of the match the fans typically remained on the terraces, singing and chanting my name. It was an emotional moment for me. It was our final home game, and although I didn't know it then, it was also the last time I would feel the warmth of the West Ham supporters at close range.

We were still bottom of the table, but we had games in hand on all those above us. We had four games to play – all away. It couldn't have been a harder climax to a difficult season. We had to play Sheffield Wednesday, Everton, Nottingham Forest and Liverpool in the space of fourteen days. I hoped that we would be safe by the time we visited Anfield, because the chances were that Liverpool would need to win that game to remain in the title race.

When we faced Wednesday, we were without Brady,

Devonshire, McAvennie and, of course, the long-term injury victims like Robson and Stewart. We won 2–0 with goals from Dickens and Rosenior. We then met Everton at Goodison Park and lost 3–1, but if we won our last two games we could still stay in Division One.

Brady was back in the side for the game againt Nottingham Forest. Leroy scored one of the fastest goals of the season after just nineteen seconds, and then added a second to clinch a 2–1 victory. It was one of our best wins of the season.

The final game was at Anfield and, just as I suspected, Liverpool needed the three points to keep the pressure on Arsenal in the Championship race. We had to win to stay up. If Liverpool won, they needed only to draw their final game against Arsenal to win the title again.

We battled and matched them for an hour, in front of a 41,855 crowd at Anfield. At half-time it was 1–1, Leroy Rosenior having scored our goal. Throughout the match I felt we had a chance of winning. And we had to win, a draw wasn't good enough. As the game wore on we pushed into those areas of greater risk, looking for the winning goal. Liverpool exploited the space we left at the back and finally won 5–1. I couldn't complain. The players had given everything they had, and they had been beaten by a superb team. The final scoreline was an unrealistic reflection of the ebb and flow of the game, but the reality was that West Ham would be playing in Division Two the following season.

I went into the Anfield boot-room at the end and received the usual commiserations from their coaching staff. They were sorry it was us. Once again, Liverpool had been the big hurdle. We stayed in a Liverpool hotel that night. We would normally have driven home, but it was the last match of the season and I had hoped it might be a night for the lads to celebrate.

I was bitterly disappointed. So, too, were the players. You can't complain, though, if you have played all your games and failed. There were mitigating circumstances, but I was never a manager who liked to offer excuses for defeat and failure. I would rather think to the future and work to put it right. Eddie Baily and I had already discussed the following season. Whether we survived in Division One or were relegated, there were two players we decided to bid for that summer. But that is now in the past.

I went home to think about the new season. It was going to be a busy summer for me. Apart from anything else, I had to discuss my new contract with the club. One day I had a call from the chairman.

'John, could you come round and see me?' he asked. 'There's something I want to discuss with you.'

'Okay, Mr Len,' I said.

THE FUTURE

Thirty-four years a working man ... and then, suddenly, I became an unemployment statistic. It took me perhaps a day to come to terms with my new life. You get only one life, and I want to try to make the most of mine.

The years at West Ham are now behind me. They are history. I am not bitter about what happened. I have no regrets. West Ham remain for me a great club of tradition and principle, and I trust that those qualities will be preserved in the years ahead. I am a shareholder of the club – Mr Len gave me a single share some years ago – with a right to vote at the annual general meeting, and I have a genuine interest in the club's well-being.

I still have many friends at Upton Park, and throughout the summer I met and spoke with many of the people who worked with me. 'How are you, John?' was inevitably the first question I heard when picking up the telephone. It is still a caring game.

The truth is, I'm fine and enjoying my new life. I spent my first long break in thirty-four years either gardening, climbing up a ladder or fishing. We have always been a close family, and we enjoyed the time together, Yvonne, Murray and I. I decided to make the best use of each day. Yvonne and I know there will be a day when I go back into football. We both know I'll go back. You can't be involved in football for thirty-four years and then just say: 'I don't want to do it anymore.' At least I can't. Marvellous as it was to be at home, I have to admit that if someone asked me to take a group of players – any players – for a training session, I'd have been as happy as a sandboy.

I have had offers of jobs, and when the right offer comes along I will go back. I have retained close contact with the game, and each Saturday since the start of the season I have been scouting for one club or other.

I was flattered to be asked, as the representative of the Football League Executive Staffs Association, to sit on the appeals tribunal that determines transfer fees in disputed cases. It was a stimulating experience, and I found the inner workings of the appeals committee fascinating. I also made new friends – notably Professor Sir John Wood, chairman of the committee.

An academic associated with the Faculty of Law at Sheffield University, and a Huddersfield Town supporter, Sir John acts as the arbitrator, finding a sensible compromise in the same way that he does for ACAS in industrial disputes.

He's not a football man in the professional sense, but he's superbly read in the game and is delightfully shrewd when dealing with chairmen, managers or players. The committee, first set up in 1978, comprises four men, and includes a Football League official and either Gordon Taylor or Brendan Batson from the Professional Footballers' Association. We listen, first, to what the player involved in the case has to say, and then we listen to the presentations from the two clubs. The selling club is invariably asking for far more cash than the buying club is prepared to pay. We have to decide on the player's valuation.

I was involved on the committee that determined Neil Webb's fee for his transfer from Nottingham Forest to Manchester United. Forest wanted £2.5 million for him. United had offered £900,000. It was intriguing listening to Sir John sift the salient facts from the evidence presented by Brian Clough's club Nottingham Forest, and Alex Ferguson's club, Manchester United. It was all conducted in a sane and dignified manner.

Of course, among the most important determining factors are the player's age and his experience. In Webb's case, he was 26, an established England international and a player of high reputation. We decided that United should pay £1.5 million, which was, at the time, the highest fee between English clubs settled by the committee.

That case was considered no more or less important, and given no more or less time and thought, than any of the dozens involving players valued at £20,000. I have been impressed with the way the system works, particularly with the diligence with which the committee members seek to reach a fair and impartial conclusion. There has to be some form of arbitration in cases where clubs can't agree a fee, and I believe the appeals committee works well, despite the occasional complaint from a disgruntled club.

My enforced break gave me plenty of time to reflect on the game and what the future holds for the world's most popular sport. Over the years, I have come to believe that the English game suffers from insularity, which is perhaps characteristic of an island race. We have to be very aware of what is happening in the rest of the footballing world, particularly with the continuing UEFA ban on the participation of English clubs in European competitions. That suspension, imposed after the Heysel Stadium riot at the Liverpool v. Juventus European Cup Final in 1985, has done little to broaden the education and experience of English players. Apart from those good enough to be selected to play for their countries, the players today have little chance to test themselves against the best in Europe.

I have always been in favour of the controlled import of foreign players into the Football League. I feel that players like the Dutchmen Frans Thijssen and Arnold Muhren, and the Argentinians Ossie Ardiles and Ricardo Villa, brought a new dimension and freshness to the First Division. They learned from us, and we learned from them, and I think it essential that the game continues to encourage contracts of this type.

At West Ham we used to have players and coaches from all over the world watching the training and working with us. One of the big Japanese clubs, Furakawa, sent two players for two months' coaching every year throughout the eighties. Some of them were top-quality Japanese internationals. They wanted to learn about the English game. They joined the training, took notes, and in the afternoons attended language schools.

I was delighted to help spread the English game to the far corners of the world, but sometimes I think we have a slightly superior attitude to the game. The Football Association, for instance, deploys English coaches throughout the Third World – and that is to be admired. But I would like to see English coaches travelling round the world not just to teach, but to learn, too. We must keep pace with the European game and examine the progress being made in South America, Africa and the Far East. We must do more to learn about changing styles and patterns of play in the rest of the world. I think England's three consecutive defeats in the 1988 European Championships in West Germay were a warning shot. Bobby Robson, the England manager, quite rightly stressed the need for greater contact with the European game after that tournament.

One of the problems, of course, in England is simply the weight of domestic fixtures and the fact that coaches and managers have little free time in which to study foreign coaching methods. For that reason, I would like us to utilize some of the respected senior figures in the game like Ron Greenwood, Bill Nicholson and Lawrie McMenemy. This would do the game in England an invaluable service, by allowing them simply to observe foreign coaching techniques, pool their ideas and report back to the main body of coaches and managers in England.

I suspect, though, that the game is too concerned at the moment with the problems in its own backyard. The biggest single issue for the major clubs in the near future concerns the existence of the Football League as we know it and the continuing threat of a breakaway superleague.

Most leagues in Europe are now dominated by the two or three richest clubs, and in many countries the superleague could evolve naturally in the next few years. I think it inevitable that the clubs with the deepest financial resources emerge at the top of the pile. For me the question is this: do the richest clubs have the right to keep most of the money they generate and the right to generate as much as they can? Or do they have a moral responsibility to the smaller clubs on their leagues? The small clubs, in England at least, have been an essential part of the life-blood of the game. I don't think the big Football League clubs will desert them totally.

But I think the time will come when the little clubs realize the benefits of running on a part-time basis, with costs cut and grounds shared. Certainly, there would be some advantages for youngsters in playing part-time. A player of 19 or 20, unsure whether he will make the grade with a big club, would almost certainly feel more secure with a smaller club where he could train and play part-time and learn a trade. He could still develop into an international-class player, as Alan Devonshire did at West Ham after working in a factory and playing for Southall until the age of 21.

I think we need to protect the small clubs, just as we need to protect the rights of the big clubs. One area where all clubs should unite is in improving the safety and comfort of spectators at matches. I would like to see more, and bigger, family areas introduced at clubs, and I would like to see them all open to visiting families. Segregation has been necessary for recent generations of fans but how good it would be for today's children to grow up alongside children from visiting clubs. In ten years' time those children would know of no other way of watching the game.

All clubs, quite rightly, are now very safety-conscious, and I believe that legislation should be introduced that ensures a specified percentage of a club's revenue is spent on non-profit-making schemes that improve the comfort of supporters on the terraces. Fortunes have been spent installing executive boxes – financially very lucrative for clubs – but it is time that more consideration was given to the fan on the terraces.

The advantage of legislation is that it guarantees an investment in spectator comfort. A football-club manager would inevitably press his board of directors to invest in new players, but I accept that there has to be a balance. Legislation deflects any boardroom conflict over how the cash is spent.

For similar reasons I would like to see each club board appoint a technical director, a man who works closely with the manager. Football is a passionate game, and when a manager wants to buy a player to help win a title or avoid relegation his emotional commitment is not always shared by the board. A technical director, preferably a former professional player, would be a great ally to any manager, in the way that Bobby Charlton must be invaluable to Alex Ferguson at Manchester United. They both share a professional's passion for the game, and Bobby, I suspect, helps give the Old Trafford boardroom a football balance at a time when the finanacial side of the game is becoming more dominant.

During my years as West Ham manager, I accepted that the club had to be run like a business. I didn't want the club to go into debt. But I didn't have a passion for the financial side of the game. There are plenty of financial men on the boards of most clubs, but it is also important that we don't lose sight of the football man's wishes.

I think one area of football finance that needs to be tightened concerns the growth of agents and the influence they now wield in some transfers. The commercialization of the game has encouraged the spread of agents, representing managers as well as players, throughout the game.

I think we have to accept that in today's increasingly commercial football world there has to be a role for financial advisers. Many players believe they need advice when negotiating with clubs, and I can understand that. It is a short career and the player wants the best deal he can get. When he retires he still has another half of his life to live, and I think good advice can help secure the future for a player. The broad terms of a contract between a club and player are often agreed quite simply. Where an adviser can help most is in suggesting to the player how he can best invest his salary in something like pension funds or building societies.

The abolition of the players' maximum wage in 1961, for which the modern player should be grateful to the negotiating skills and perseverance of Jimmy Hill, opened a new era in the game. The salaries of players suddenly leapt. Johnny Haynes, of Fulham and England, was the first to earn £100 a week. I was a youngster at Upton Park at the time and, before the removal of the maximum wage limit, the most the senior players earned was £20 a week.

Modern-day salaries have been further enhanced by freedom of contract. These days a player becomes a free agent when his contract expires and, if his club wants to keep him, they must offer new terms no less favourable than those he had previously. It can be a problem for some clubs if a handful of players are out of contract at the end of the same season. I always tried to have my established players at West Ham on three- or four-year contracts, and I tried to ensure that no more than three or four were out of contract at the same time. I've heard of cases where clubs have had ten players out of contract at the same time – an enormous headache for a manager trying to plan for a new season.

At West Ham we tried to encourage and reward loyalty among senior players and provide incentives for the younger ones. I have had teams at West Ham in which a youngster was on a basic £150 a week, while a senior player was on a basic in excess of £1,000. The young player, of course, would receive a further 50 per cent in appearance money. At that stage in his career the appearance bonus would act as an incentive for him to try to establish himself in the first team.

I always tried to be fair and honest with my players, and I think they appreciated it. Some, even on the point of their departure to another club, would ask my advice about the offer they had received. I remember Paul Goddard asking what I thought of Newcastle's offer to him when we agreed to sell him to them for £425,000 in November 1986. He wasn't sure that he wanted to leave Upton Park and I certainly didn't want to lose him.

But he wanted regular first-team football, and he couldn't get into the side because of the form of Tony Cottee and Frank McAvennie. He had a year of his contract to run and I had just offered him improved terms. It was a good offer, and he was quoted in the newspapers at the time as saying he considered it a very generous offer. I'd told him of Newcastle's interest, because that was my policy. If you don't tell a player a club has made an enquiry, they will only learn about it from another source.

Paul talked to the Newcastle manager, Willie McFaul, and what appealed to him was the chance of a regular first-team place. None the less, their offer to him was good, too. What should he do? When he asked me I told him: 'It's a marvellous offer, and it shows, in my opinion, that they have great respect for you as a footballer and they want you in their first team.' I didn't want him to go, but I had to be honest with him. I think he was grateful for the advice.

The nuts and bolts of that deal were quite straightforward, though nowadays, with clubs employing financial directors and players increasingly seeking guidance from advisers, transfer negotiations are becoming more complex. I remember the day in 1977 when I bought Derek Hales from Derby County. I called Tommy Docherty, then the manager at the Baseball

Ground, and told him that I would like to buy Derek. 'It's £100,000,' said Tom.

'Fine,' I said. The deal was agreed in two minutes.

I always started negotiations with a club manager, but nowadays a financial director, chief executive or, in some cases, the club chairman is likely to be involved before a deal is agreed. I understand the need for this, but I always preferred to complete my transfers as quickly and quietly as possible. The more people who know your intentions, the greater the chance of your interest leaking out and a rival stepping in to snatch the player away from you or increase the asking price. Occasionally, if I noticed in a newspaper that a player I admired was available, I might ask one of my senior players at West Ham for an opinion. They might have once played at the same club together or been in an international squad together. For the most part, though, I like to keep my transfer plans close to my chest.

Of course, it can sometimes be to a player's benefit if several clubs, rather than just one or two, are interested in signing him. The player's advisers are, of course, often quite happy to make a number of clubs aware of their client's availability. This is an area the Football League is concerned about. They have formed a committee to consider the role of agents, specifically relating to their involvement in transfers. They have looked at sports in America where, in many cases, agents have to be licensed by governing bodies of sports.

I think we should also look deeper into the American treatment of injured sportsmen and the methods used to enhance recovery rates. Since Angela Cannell joined West Ham as a physiologist, I have realized that there is a vast reservoir of information available from around the world on the training and treatment of sportsmen.

I was impressed by the way Angela applied her knowledge in football. The speed of football has outgrown most other facets in the evolution of the game, and as a direct consequence of this players are becoming increasingly susceptible to stress injuries, particularly in the pelvic region. Many clubs, unless they are very lucky, could be without four or five experienced first-team players because of injury at any one time. Ten years ago you felt you were unlucky if you had two players absent through injury.

I think football has to look closely at the training techniques employed, to ensure that we are doing the best for the players. Coaches might be experts with a football, but there are other specialists with greater knowledge of fitness levels. If a team loses 5–0, the manager's reaction is often emotive. 'I'll work them harder in training,' he says. That is not always the answer. A fitness expert would probably think differently. Football needs to do more research on fitness levels, particularly on how much training a player should do during the week to ensure he's at his peak on a Saturday afternoon.

One day at Chadwell Heath, before I left West Ham, Angela was watching the players sprinting when she pointed out the young full back Steve Potts, and said that within two minutes he would pull a hamstring. Within thirty seconds of her saying that, Steve was rubbing his hamstring between sprints. We pulled him out of the session and her assistant stretched out his hamstring and then sent him for a run around the perimeter of the training ground. When he returned he was fine.

Had she not spotted that sudden alteration in his running pattern, Steve Potts would have pulled his hamstring and been ruled out of action for a fortnight. That incident underlined to me the importance of getting the balance right in training and, specifically, the importance of stretching exercises before and after rigorous training.

What I have learned in my thirty-four years at West Ham is that the game is constantly evolving; that is the fascination of it. And that is the challenge for someone like me. I have always thrived on a challenge. The day I left West Ham I vowed I would be back. And I will.

Football is in my blood. The game goes on, and I like to feel I am still part of it. I enjoyed my years at West Ham, and many friendships still endure, but I want to look to the future. For me the bubbles will never fade and die completely. You cannot devote thirty-four years to one club and not still retain some kind of affection.

But those years are memories, and mostly happy memories. What does the future hold for me? Who can be sure. I think I emerged from Upton Park with my reputation intact. I was flattered and honoured to be asked by the England manager, Bobby Robson, to help assess possible World Cup opponents before the 1990 Finals in Italy.

It was good to be involved in the game at such an elevated level. But, like most club managers, I dream of competing for the big domestic prizes, like the League Championship and the FA Cup. The League Championship was the one major honour that eluded us at West Ham. I would relish the challenge of another crack at it.

For me, competing is as important as winning. But it would be nice one day, who knows where, who knows when, to hold that League Championship trophy aloft – just like my dreams.

INDEX

References in *italic* indicate illustration(s)
between pages indicated

FOR THE BEST IN PAPERBACKS, LOOK FOR THE

In every corner of the world, on every subject under the sun, Penguin represents quality and variety – the very best in publishing today.

For complete information about books available from Penguin – including Puffins, Penguin Classics and Arkana – and how to order them, write to us at the appropriate address below. Please note that for copyright reasons the selection of books varies from country to country.

In the United Kingdom: Please write to *Dept E.P., Penguin Books Ltd, Harmondsworth, Middlesex, UB7 0DA.*

If you have any difficulty in obtaining a title, please send your order with the correct money, plus ten per cent for postage and packaging, to *PO Box No 11, West Drayton, Middlesex*

In the United States: Please write to *Dept BA, Penguin, 299 Murray Hill Parkway, East Rutherford, New Jersey 07073*

In Canada: Please write to *Penguin Books Canada Ltd, 2801 John Street, Markham, Ontario L3R 1B4*

In Australia: Please write to the *Marketing Department, Penguin Books Australia Ltd, P.O. Box 257, Ringwood, Victoria 3134*

In New Zealand: Please write to the *Marketing Department, Penguin Books (NZ) Ltd, Private Bag, Takapuna, Auckland 9*

In India: Please write to *Penguin Overseas Ltd, 706 Eros Apartments, 56 Nehru Place, New Delhi, 110019*

In the Netherlands: Please write to *Penguin Books Netherlands B.V., Postbus 195, NL–1380AD Weesp*

In West Germany: Please write to *Penguin Books Ltd, Friedrichstrasse 10–12, D–6000 Frankfurt/Main 1*

In Spain: Please write to *Longman Penguin España, Calle San Nicolas 15, E–28013 Madrid*

In Italy: Please write to *Penguin Italia s.r.l., Via Como 4, I-20096 Pioltello (Milano)*

In France: Please write to *Penguin Books Ltd, 39 Rue de Montmorency, F-75003 Paris*

In Japan: Please write to *Longman Penguin Japan Co Ltd, Yamaguchi Building, 2-12-9 Kanda Jimbocho, Chiyoda-Ku, Tokyo 101*

FOR THE BEST IN PAPERBACKS, LOOK FOR THE 🐧

PENGUIN BESTSELLERS

The New Confessions William Boyd

The outrageous, hilarious autobiography of John James Todd, a Scotsman born in 1899 and one of the great self-appointed (and failed) geniuses of the twentieth century. 'Brilliant ... a Citizen Kane of a novel' – *Daily Telegraph*

The House of Stairs Barbara Vine

'A masterly and hypnotic synthesis of past, present and terrifying future ... compelling and disturbing' – *Sunday Times*. 'Not only ... a quietly smouldering suspense novel but also ... an accurately atmospheric portrayal of London in the heady '60s. Literally unputdownable' – *Time Out*

Summer's Lease John Mortimer

'It's high summer, high comedy too, when Molly drags her amiably bickering family to a rented Tuscan villa for the hols ... With a cosy fluency of wit, Mortimer charms us into his urbane tangle of clues...' – *Mail on Sunday*. 'Superb' – Ruth Rendell

Touch Elmore Leonard

'I bleed from five wounds and heal people, but I've never been in love. Isn't that something?' They call him Juvenal, and he's a wanted man in downtown Detroit... 'Discover Leonard for yourself – he's something else' – *Daily Mail*

Story of My Life Jay McInerney

'The first year I was in New York I didn't do anything but guys and blow...' 'The leader of the pack' – *Time Out*. 'Fast and sharp ... a very good novel indeed' – *Observer*

FOR THE BEST IN PAPERBACKS, LOOK FOR THE 🐧

BIOGRAPHY AND AUTOBIOGRAPHY IN PENGUIN

Just for William   Nicholas Woolley and Sue Clayton

Originating as a film for the award-winning BBC2 documentary series *Forty Minutes*, *Just for William* is the story of William Clayton, diagnosed with leukaemia at the age of nine – and the story of a family who refused to give up hope in the battle against one of the deadliest diseases of all.

The Secret Lives of Trebitsch Lincoln   Bernard Wasserstein

Trebitsch Lincoln was Member of Parliament, international spy, right-wing revolutionary, Buddhist monk – and this century's most extra-ordinary conman. 'An utterly improbable story … a biographical scoop' – *Guardian*

Tolstoy   A. N. Wilson

'One of the best biographies of our century' – Leon Edel. 'All his skills as a writer, his fire as a critic, his insight as a novelist and his experience of life have come together in this subject' – Peter Levi in the *Independent*

Fox on the Run   Graeme Fowler

The intimate diary of a dramatic eighteen months, in which Fowler became the first Englishman to score a double century in India – before being cast down by injury and forced to come to terms with loss of form. 'One of the finest cricket books this year' – *Yorkshire Post*. Winner of the first Observer/Running Late Sports Book Award.

Backcloth   Dirk Bogarde

The final volume of Dirk Bogarde's autobiography is not about his acting years but about Dirk Bogarde the man and the people and events that have shaped his life and character. All are remembered with affection, nostalgia and characteristic perception and eloquence.

Jackdaw Cake   Norman Lewis

From Carmarthen to Cuba, from Enfield to Algeria, Norman Lewis brilliantly recounts his transformation from stammering schoolboy to the man Auberon Waugh called 'the greatest travel writer alive, if not the greatest since Marco Polo'.